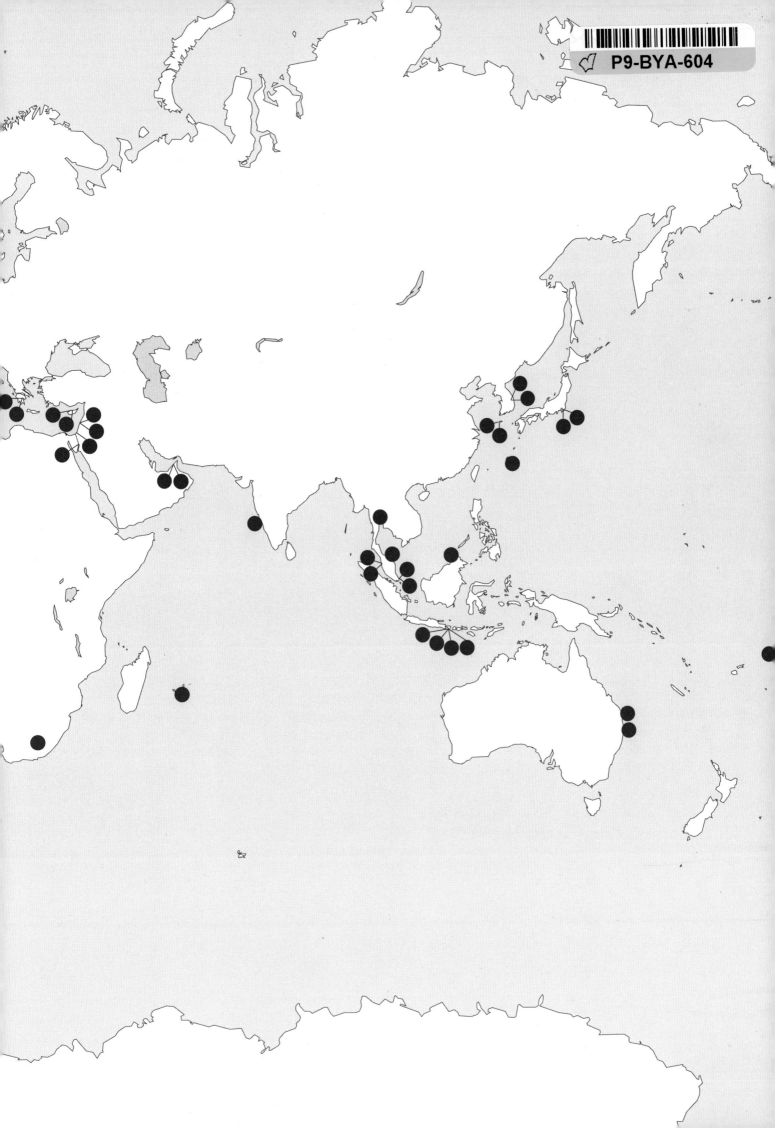

P9-BYA-604

DESIGNING THE WORLD'S BEST

RESORTS

WIMBERLY ALLISON TONG & GOO

Second reprint 2002
(The Images Publishing Group Reference Number: 502)

First reprint 2001

First published in Australia in 2001 by
The Images Publishing Group Pty Ltd
ACN 059 734 431
6 Bastow Place, Mulgrave, Victoria, 3170, Australia
Telephone: (+61 3) 9561 5544 Facsimile (+61 3) 9561 4860
Email: books@images.com.au
Website: www.imagespublishinggroup.com

Copyright © The Images Publishing Group Pty Ltd 2001
The Images Publishing Group Reference Number: 472

All rights reserved. Apart from any fair dealing for the purposes
of private study, research, criticism or review as permitted under the
Copyright Act, no part of this publication may be reproduced, stored in
a retrieval system or transmitted in any form by any means, electronic,
mechanical, photocopying, recording or otherwise, without the written
permission of the publisher.

National Library of Australia Cataloguing-in-Publication Data

Wimberly Allison Tong & Goo (Firm).
Designing the World's Best Resorts.

Includes index.
ISBN 1 86470 073 4.

1. Resort architecture. 2. Resorts – Design and
Construction. 3. Hotels – Design and Construction.
4. Architecture and Recreation. I. Title.

728.5

Edited by Howard J. Wolff
Designed by The Graphic Image Studio Pty Ltd
Mulgrave, Australia

Film by Mission Productions Limited, Hong Kong

Printed by Everbest Printing Co. Ltd., Hong Kong/China

IMAGES has included on its website a page for special notices in relation to this and
our other publications. It includes updates to the information printed in our books.
Please visit this site: www.imagespublishinggroup.com

DESIGNING THE WORLD'S BEST
RESORTS

WIMBERLY ALLISON TONG & GOO

images
Publishing

Preface

By the senior leaders of Wimberly Allison Tong & Goo

We were honored to be asked by The Images Publishing Group to share the story of Wimberly Allison Tong & Goo (WATG) through the resorts that we have designed over the last five decades. Honored and overwhelmed.

Beginning with the renovation of the Royal Hawaiian hotel in 1945, we made an early decision to specialize. Today, WATG has designed more hotels and resorts than any other firm on the planet, having worked on projects in 119 countries across six continents. The task of choosing 'the best' of these is akin to being asked as a parent, 'Which of your children do you love the most?'

More than just a collection of pretty pictures, the projects highlighted here were selected to reflect evolving trends in international travel and noteworthy preferences on the part of resort guests and owners. They also illustrate how destinations can satisfy the desire for rejuvenation, recreation, romance, excitement, escape, and enrichment.

Our projects take their inspiration from the qualities that make their locations unique.

George 'Pete' Wimberly, the firm's founder, was creating architecture with a strong sense of place long before it was fashionable. And we're still heeding the principle of cultural authenticity.

We've expanded the idea of 'sense of place' to include places that exist only in the imagination; lost cultures and created myths invite us to explore history as it might have been. We think of our job as not just designing buildings but as scripting experiences.

The result, we hope, is a body of work that no longer renders the predictable acceptable. As different as WATG projects are from one another, our goal for each one is explicitly communicated in our firm's mission: to responsibly create special environments that lift the spirit.

Of course, none of our work would be possible without the vision and knowledge of clients who understand what people want and how to give it to them. The world's best resorts are those that please their owners by pleasing the people who stay there, work there, and live nearby.

Claridge's: An urban resort renovated by WATG
London, England, UK
Photography: Courtesy of Claridge's

Contents

Contents continued

Introduction

By Mary Scoviak

For more than 50 years, Wimberly Allison Tong & Goo (WATG) has not been following trends; it has been setting them.

Rejecting the idea that a hotel has to look functional to be functional, WATG has deconstructed the old notions about what made a hotel or resort popular and profitable. WATG stopped seeing architecture as a barrier and rethought it as a strategic interface between the world without and the world within. What WATG has taught guests, managers, and investors is that different is better, and that memorable is better still.

By infusing each of its projects with a sense of place, WATG's architects, planners, and designers create hotels and resorts that are experiences in themselves. The firm's talented staff draws on the best of local culture to immerse guests in an atmosphere that constantly reminds them of where they are and why they have come.

By marrying its own technical expertise and vast hotel experience with the wisdom of local builders, WATG has opened up new worlds for travelers—worlds as diverse as elegant, thatched-roof island resorts; white stucco retreats along the sea; chic casinos; meccas of urban entertainment; and palaces that blur created myth with sumptuous reality.

Exceeding guest expectations is an important element of successful design, but it is only one aspect. To be truly successful, a project must enhance the revenue opportunities for the manager and drive return on investment for the owner.

The combination of elegant, exciting aesthetics with a hard-working, efficient framework has a major impact on profit potential. Discerning travelers consistently rank WATG-designed hotels among the top in the world. Equally important, studies show that WATG's hotels and resorts typically maintain substantial rate premiums within their competitive set. Good architecture and design have driven up gross operating profits by double- and sometimes triple-digit figures following comprehensive renovation and repositioning. These are the palpable financial indicators of how successful WATG's approach has been and what a chord it has struck with the traveling public.

The measure of the success of WATG's visionary take on architecture and design lies in the long-lasting appeal of its hotel and resort work. Looking over the 75 projects featured in this book, it is difficult to assign a date to the properties. The designs are unique, timeless, yet detailed enough to be 'new' each time the guest returns. Whether in cities, on islands or, one day soon, under the sea, WATG's projects expand our horizons and remind us that creativity has no limitations.

The Palace of The Lost City
Sun City, South Africa
Photography: Courtesy of Sun International

Mary Scoviak is design editor for HOTELS *magazine, executive editor of* Hotels' Investment Outlook *and author of* International Hotel and Resort Design.

Destination Resorts

Anatomy of a Destination
by Michael S. Rubin, PhD

Today most of our leisure time is given over to amusements, to a hiatus from the work-a-day world. Yet the longing for the good life, for personal renewal, for enrichment and discovery, has never been greater. In an age in which every place is electronically accessible but remote from our touch, we seek remote places that offer access to new perspectives, discoveries, and encounters.

Creating a destination—a setting for leisure and renewal—is, therefore, a special kind of place-making. The destination is first and foremost an imagined place, an ideal experience we hope for in the future and cherish from the past. As an ideal place, the destination cannot simply be appreciated passively but requires participation in an experience that is, by definition, transitory. Physically and psychologically, the guest must leave a familiar world of routines to enter a novel realm of discovery and renewal. It is inevitable that the guest will eventually return to that world, but with the possibility that the place visited will provide a transformative experience.

For over half a century, Wimberly Allison Tong & Goo has been on the leading edge of destination architecture. This is not simply because the firm has designed more resorts than any other firm—quantity must take a back seat to quality in the architecture of destinations. Nor is it due to the fact that the firm has specialized in hospitality and leisure projects. It is that WATG has developed an architectural language that infuses destinations with a promise of transformation for their visitors.

Michael Rubin is president of MRA International and chairman of MRA Eventures, specializing in entertainment-based development.

Grand Hyatt Bali
Nusa Dua, Bali, Indonesia
Photography: Donna Day

The Royal Hawaiian

Waikiki Beach, Honolulu, Oahu, Hawaii, USA

The Royal Hawaiian, affectionately known as the 'Pink Palace of the Pacific,' is an historic landmark on the world's most famous beach.

In 1945, owners of the Royal Hawaiian decided to restore the famed hotel, which opened its doors in 1927, to its pre-Second World War eminence. At the time, it was one of only two hotels in Waikiki. As WATG's first commission, the project launched the firm into an area of expertise and a commitment to cultural authenticity that continue to this day.

With its famous pink façade, vaulted Spanish archways, classical elegance, and spectacular beachfront location, the hotel has been host to eight decades of guests and retains its legendary stature.

It is situated on the former site of the royal coconut grove and summer home of Queen Kaahumanu. Guestrooms are spacious and offer the old-world charm of high ceilings, along with all of today's modern amenities.

The Royal Hawaiian remains a favorite of many travelers; the hotel was chosen by readers of *Travel + Leisure* magazine as one of the 'Best Hotels in the World' and among the top 10 'Best Hotels in Hawaii.'

Client:	Matson Hotel Company
Site Size:	15 acres
Project Size:	349 guestrooms and suites
Amenities:	Seaside restaurant; bar; 68,000 square feet of ballroom and function rooms; garden lanai; 10,000-square-foot outdoor-function garden; freshwater pool

Grand Hyatt Bali

Nusa Dua, Bali, Indonesia

One of the greatest challenges in designing this full-service luxury resort and retail complex was to do so without overwhelming the terrain and culture of its island location.

Patterned after a Balinese village, the resort buildings are organized into four decentralized clusters with their own courtyards and separate themes; all are connected by lighted, landscaped pathways to the main lobby village. In accordance with the local edict, none of the structures exceeds the height of a coconut tree (49 feet).

The lobby/reception building derives its architectural character from the Balinese water palace; and waterfalls, pools, lagoons, and lotus ponds throughout the property reinforce this experience.

Amenities are spread among the landscaped grounds, including restaurants with varied ethnic menus, Balinese street markets, boutiques, a theater, and a Hindu temple. The Galleria Retail/Cultural Center offers a cultural shopping experience, which includes craft demonstrations, Balinese performances, and exhibits.

Though steeped in timeless Balinese traditions, the Grand Hyatt Bali is digitally wired to the world and, with its large convention center, was named the 'Best Resort Hotel Worldwide' by *Business Traveler* magazine.

Client:	P.T. Wynncor
Site Size:	40 acres (hotel); 27 acres (retail/cultural complex)
Project Size:	750 guestrooms, including 35 suites and four deluxe villas; 248,000-square-foot retail/cultural complex
Amenities:	Indonesian food court; fitness center; tennis courts; squash courts; beach club; three swimming pools; business center; conference facilities

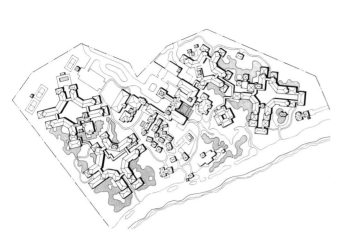

Grand Hyatt Bali

The Ritz-Carlton, Naples

Naples, Florida, USA

Voted by *Travel + Leisure* readers as the 'Best Hotel in the Continental United States and Canada' and second 'Best Hotel and Resort in the World,' as well as recipient of the Zagat Award for 'Best United States Resort,' The Ritz-Carlton, Naples is often credited with putting Naples on the map and ushering in a new era of tourism.

The hotel features twin belvedere towers, gracefully arched windows, an arcade with classic balustrades of molded stone—all reminiscent of the monumental villas of Italy and late nineteenth century hotels of Florida, which reflected their Italian legacy.

The 14-story tower leaves room on the relatively narrow site for terrace landscaping, English rose gardens, seven tennis courts, a breezy veranda, a swimming pool, and beachside restaurant. The building's U-shape, with guest wings perpendicular to the strand, gives every guestroom an ocean view.

Rich materials and lavish proportions in the public areas of the hotel replay the architectural theme of a timeless, classically scaled design. Off the two-level lobby, a grand staircase climbs to the mezzanine. All habitable spaces are at least 13 feet above the natural grade for flood control, and a delicate ecosystem of wetlands was carefully protected.

Client: W.B. Johnson Properties, Inc.
Site Size: 20 beachfront acres
Project Size: 463 guestrooms, including 28 suites
Amenities: Health club; seven tennis courts; swimming pool; formal gardens; 35,000 square feet of meeting and banquet space; nine restaurants and lounges

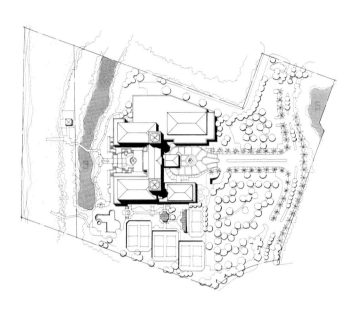

The Ritz-Carlton, Naples

Naples, Florida, USA

Hyatt Regency Maui Resort & Spa

Kaanapali Beach Resort, Lahaina, Maui, Hawaii, USA

The Hyatt Regency Maui Resort & Spa overlooks an intricate system of waterfalls, pools, and lagoons, which meander and cascade through elaborate tropical and Japanese gardens.

The hotel occupies an 18.5-acre beachfront property on the Kaanapali Coast of Maui. Constructed amenities that relate to the island's natural attractions —such as waterfalls, lagoons, and landscaped gardens— combine to make the Hyatt Regency Maui Resort & Spa one of the world's first fantasy resorts.

The complex includes three mid-rise buildings with broad views of the expansive pools and gardens below and the Pacific Ocean in the background. Native woods as well as regional artwork and sculpture help to create a tropical environment that is simultaneously elegant and informal.

The hotel's main ballroom, dining, and entertainment areas were renovated to create a Hawaiian-themed décor, involving extensive use of koa wood and hand-painted ceiling murals.

Readers of *Gourmet* magazine selected the Hyatt Regency Maui Resort & Spa as the 'Best Hotel in Hawaii.'

Client:	Maui Development Company
Site Size:	18.5 beachfront acres
Project Size:	815 guestrooms and suites
Amenities:	43,560-square-foot swimming pool; lagoons; tennis courts; shopping and dining promenades; health club; meeting rooms; 17,000-square-foot ballroom

Hotel Lotte Cheju Resort

Cheju Island, South Korea

Hotel Lotte Cheju Resort is designed to be a 'Palace of Dreams' in a semi-tropical setting that offers luxury, recreation, and entertainment.

Built upon the shores of beautiful Cheju Island, long known for its breathtaking views of the ocean and Mount Halla, along with lush green forests and rocky red cliffs formed by ancient volcanoes, Hotel Lotte Cheju Resort incorporates the natural beauty of its location and creates its own ambiance of leisure and luxury, recreation and fun.

The big design challenge was the site—a deep valley leading to the sea. The hotel building, which incorporates design forms derived from traditional Korean architecture, cascades down one side of the valley, while elegant 'farmhouse' villa suites are perched on the other side. Public areas are sited on a plateau at the head of the valley.

The resort includes a variety of room types to fit guest preferences, including 125 rooms designed especially for families. In addition, Hotel Lotte Cheju Resort caters to business travelers, with conference rooms that can

accommodate 1,000 people and banquet facilities equipped with an eight-language simultaneous translation system.

Within the resort's palatial setting, guests can enjoy spectacular views and landscapes and a wide range of dining options with Korean, Japanese, and Western menus. In addition to a variety of recreational facilities on site, the resort features a themed water show, boating on the artificial lake, a volcano, animated dragon fountain, and a series of windmills reminiscent of the Netherlands.

Client:	Hotel Lotte Co. Ltd.
Site Size:	21 acres
Project Size:	500 guestrooms
Amenities:	Conference and banquet facilities; casino; duty-free shop; fitness club; swimming pool; tennis court; family recreation center; nearby facilities for golf and ocean sports

The Ritz-Carlton, Laguna Niguel

Dana Point, California, USA

The Ritz-Carlton, Laguna Niguel's extraordinary location on a 150-foot-high bluff overlooking the Pacific Ocean governed design plans for the resort.

The client wanted the resort to offer an unparalleled sense of privacy and exclusivity to guests, but compliance with codes stipulated public access to the beach.

The architects chose a Spanish Mediterranean style as most suitable for the location. The design forms an 'E' with open legs extending away from the ocean to give privacy to guests and neighboring residents. Two L-shaped wings extend the sense of seclusion from inside the resort, while offering a discreet public view and access.

Due to a mandated height restriction, design plans modified the typical Spanish-style hip roof and situated the first floor 15 feet below existing grade.

The ocean was always the focal point for this design. Interior spaces are divided into comfortable, intimate settings. Colors and materials are understated to blend with the natural setting, giving the resort the appearance of a Mediterranean village melded to the bluff.

The Ritz-Carlton, Laguna Niguel has been voted the number one 'Best Hotel in the Continental United States and Canada' by *Travel + Leisure* magazine; 'Most Romantic Resort in the World' by *Gourmet* magazine; and 'Top Golf Resort in the United States' by *Successful Meetings* magazine.

Client:	W. B. Johnson Properties, Inc.
Site Size:	17.5 acres
Project Size:	393 guestrooms
Amenities:	Four tennis courts; two heated pools; fitness center; 18-hole Robert Trent Jones II golf course; eight restaurants and lounges; 2 miles of beachfront

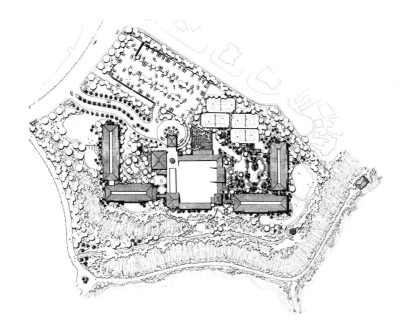

The Ritz-Carlton, Laguna Niguel

Hilton Hawaiian Village

Waikiki Beach, Honolulu, Oahu, Hawaii, USA

Without interrupting hotel operations, the architect completely rejuvenated the aging, 20-acre Hilton Hawaiian Village into a beachfront oasis in the heart of urban Waikiki.

Through a multi-phased program initiated in 1986, WATG's master plan involved creating a village around a central open space by demolishing certain buildings, renovating others, building new ones, relocating food/beverage/retail outlets, and adding major water features and extensive landscaping. The resort's many functions—retail, convention, recreation, entertainment, and hospitality—are connected by creative landscaping and a festive village atmosphere.

An outstanding example of contemporary Hawaiian architecture, the Hilton's open-air reception pavilion overlooks a progression of water views: fountains, a 10,000-square-foot free-form swimming pool, and the Pacific Ocean.

With openness as the design goal, space was reconfigured to maximize the flow between indoors and out. Created from what was semi-basement space, the hotel's redesigned coffee shop has two-story doors that open to individual dining pods overlooking a carp pool.

Most recently, WATG designed the 24-story Kalia Tower, with 453 guestrooms, a world-class spa, an exclusive Hilton Executive Lounge, and retail outlets.

Client:	Hilton Hotels Corporation
Site Size:	20 oceanfront acres
Project Size:	2,523 guestrooms
Amenities:	A village of mixed-use buildings: 10 restaurants and lounges; 100 specialty shops; 113,000 square feet of banquet and conference space; cabaret theater; lagoon; four swimming pools; health club; two luau gardens

The Leela Palace, Goa

Mobor, Goa, India

The Leela Palace, Goa was awarded the prestigious Gallivanter's Guide Award of Excellence for its 'superb layout, architectural features, elegance, and ethnic beauty.'

Designed to reflect Goa's unique heritage and geographical location, the Leela Palace, Goa combines 13th century Vijayanagara architecture with 18th century Mediterranean ambiance; its architectural style is reminiscent of the palaces of southern India. This world-class resort has a private, 984-foot expanse of white sand beach and is set amid lush gardens and lagoons overlooking the Indian Ocean.

The five-star hotel represents a complete redesign of an existing 300-room beach hotel and the addition of over 80 luxurious villa units. The pink stucco, tiled-roof one- and two-story villas feature marble bathrooms (each with a sunken tub and separate shower), hand-carved furniture and Indian art, as well as terraced balconies and, in some cases, private plunge pools.

The main entrance features natural stone corbels with engraved motifs. Bronze idols and stone-carved sculptures of mythological animals adorn the hotel's public spaces.

Whether relaxing under intricately carved friezes in the open-air pink sandstone lobby, or indulging in a regionally inspired treatment at the resort's spa, guests at the Leela Palace, Goa enjoy the melding of India's cultural heritage with world-class standards for luxury.

Client:	Hotel Leelaventure Ltd.
Site Size:	75 acres
Project Size:	159 guestrooms, including 87 suites
Amenities:	Casino; ballroom and meeting facilities; spa and fitness center; freeform swimming pool; nine-hole golf course; private plunge pools; tennis club; four restaurants

The Ritz-Carlton, Rancho Mirage

Rancho Mirage, California, USA

In a desert ringed with mountains, The Ritz-Carlton, Rancho Mirage appears to be carved from the bluff.

The architectural design of this resort was influenced by the warm, dry climate of its desert setting. Airy courtyards are abundant, and each guestroom has a balcony. Ample terraces extend from the lobby lounge, restaurants, conference facilities facing the pool, adjacent lawns, and outdoor dining areas. Pale colors temper the desert climate by reflecting heat and light; long roof overhangs and deep balconies provide shade.

As the resort is situated near the Santa Rosa Mountain refuge of the endangered bighorn sheep, a low-impact design that makes use of subtle color and stonework was developed. A Wright-influenced design concept is evident in the continuous horizontal lines and the emphatically low roof pitch of the buildings, which give center stage to the spectacular and rugged terrain that surrounds the hotel.

Condé Nast Traveler ranked The Ritz-Carlton, Rancho Mirage the 'Number One Resort in Southern California' and number 10 among the 'Top Resorts in North America.'

Client:	Partnership of Federated Development Co. and The Ritz-Carlton Hotel Co.
Site Size:	24 acres
Project Size:	219 guestrooms, including 21 suites
Amenities:	Pool and fitness center; over 10,000 square feet of meeting and banquet space; ten-court tennis facility; four restaurants and lounges

Sheraton Maui Hotel

Kaanapali Beach, Maui, Hawaii, USA

Thirty years after designing the Sheraton Maui, WATG upgraded the resort's 627,003 square feet of facilities through a combination of demolition, renovation, construction of new towers and added wings, and extensive site amenities.

The one thing that hasn't changed about the Sheraton Maui is its remarkable site, which is dominated by the lava promontory 80 feet above the beach called *Pu'u Keka'a*, or Black Rock.

In an effort to maintain the spirit of the existing hotel, five new concrete wings mimic the existing architecture with gracious curves and radiused balconies. The curvilinear design of the buildings is accentuated in the site design of walkways, water features, and other amenities.

The hub of the redevelopment is the new entry building—housing the lobby, new meeting facilities, all three restaurants, two new low-rise room wings, two freestanding bars, and a swimming pool and water feature complex.

With the lobby located on the second floor, arriving guests have dramatic views of the ocean and Black Rock.

The first hotel to be built on the Kaanapali coastline, the Sheraton Maui has been a sought-after destination for four decades. Its recent overhaul has repositioned it as a more upmarket hotel.

Client:	Kyo-ya Co., Ltd.
Site Size:	23 acres
Project Size:	510 guestrooms, including 48 suites
Amenities:	Three restaurants and three lounges; 17,000 square feet of ballroom, function and meeting space; 426-foot freshwater swimming lagoon; fitness center; three tennis courts; retail

Nikko Bali Resort & Spa

Sawangan, Bali, Indonesia

Nikko Bali Resort & Spa is situated along the Bali coastline
on a natural bluff above a dramatic limestone cliff.

The hotel's design takes full advantage of its breathtaking site and establishes a contemporary Balinese style by using traditional elements in a refined and elegant way. Balinese artwork and watercourts throughout the property, along with materials such as coral stone and a touch of red Balinese brick, link the hotel with its location.

Cliff-side guestrooms (in a variety of configurations) provide dramatic views as does the main lobby, which sits 46 feet above the turquoise waters of the Indian Ocean. Upon descending the dramatic 14-story cliff-hugging tower, guests find a secluded, private beach and stimulating esplanade that leads to surprises such as the restaurants, spa, and amphitheater.

Client:	P.T. Caterison Sukes
Site Size:	35 acres
Project Size:	398 guestrooms
Amenities:	Ballroom and meeting rooms; tennis center; Balinese watercourt; amphitheater; health spa; five international restaurants; lagoon pool

The Ritz-Carlton, St Thomas

St Thomas, US Virgin Islands

The design team set out to preserve a significant ecological site and, in the process, created a five-star destination that was rated by *Condé Nast Traveler* magazine as 'the number one resort in the Caribbean/Atlantic.'

A carefully preserved, ecologically sensitive salt pond became a major design element as six, three-story guest buildings and a separate dining facility were placed in a semicircle that borders the pond and overlooks the bay. Low-density, spacious grounds, retaining walls made up of stone taken from the site, and secluded parking help to keep the hotel's focus on its coastal setting.

All courtyards in the guestroom buildings are finished in a fossil-like stone that blends with the native landscape. Not only were materials chosen for their suitability to the site and the classical Mediterranean architecture, they also were designed to withstand hurricanes. All of the hotel's structures are of concrete masonry with operable windows for natural cooling.

The resort has its own generator and desalination plant, and waste water is recycled.

The Ritz-Carlton, St Thomas succeeds both as a world-class resort and as a development that preserves its fragile, coastal environment.

Client:	Pemberton Resorts
Site Size:	15 acres
Project Size:	148 oceanview guestrooms and four suites
Amenities:	Four restaurants and lounges; swimming pool; three tennis courts; fitness center; aquatic center; over 10,000 square feet of meeting space

The Ritz-Carlton, St Thomas

St Thomas, US Virgin Islands

Royal Mirage

Jumeirah Beach, Dubai, United Arab Emirates

Challenging the status quo of sleek, contemporary high-rise hotels in Dubai, the Royal Mirage was patterned after a traditional Arabian home.

The inspiration for the design of this resort is based on the very rich heritage of the region. Traditional Arabic themes permeate every aspect of Dubai's five-star, 250-room Royal Mirage. The quality of the architecture underscores the opulence of the Arabic culture and challenges the region's large-scale, high-rise competitors.

Thirteen hundred palm trees encircle a splendid Arabic fortress, but the lush landscaping and low-rise structures ensure that the views and the beach environment are the primary focal points. Subtle Arabic elements—such as tile floors, curving archways, and diffused lighting from lanterns and torches throughout—lend continuity to the resort. Arabian touches can even be found in each guestroom's bathing suite, complete with vaulted ceilings, gilded mirrors, and an arch framing the tub.

Courtyards, waterways, and terraces not only extend the fantasy of the Royal Mirage, but also maximize outdoor space-use options for the operator. The Royal Mirage has positioned itself as a destination resort first and foremost, but it also has the facilities and quality standards to appeal to high-end corporate travelers and to residents of Dubai, as well.

Client:	Mirage Leisure Development
Site Size:	25 acres
Project Size:	250 guestrooms and suites
Amenities:	Conference and banqueting areas; four restaurants; four lounges; chilled swimming pools; deluxe health and beauty salon

Jumeirah Beach, Dubai, United Arab Emirates

The Ritz-Carlton, Bali

Jimbaran, Bali, Indonesia

The Ritz-Carlton, Bali property perches dramatically on a bluff overlooking the Indian Ocean and offers guests the privacy of secluded, white sand beaches.

Bali's traditional architecture and natural beauty abound in the resort's 173 acres of lily ponds, sculptured fountains, and tiered lawns reminiscent of terraced rice paddies.

Guests can choose between accommodations in the four-story central building or the one-, two-, and three-bedroom villas on site. The *alang-alang* thatched roof villas offer ocean-view plunge pools with infinity edges, and each includes a *bale bengong*, a traditional open-air lounging area.

The hotel's sensitivity to Balinese design can be seen in the low-rise massing and in details such as thatched roofing, brightly colored Balinese doors, limestone carvings, intricately woven mats, slate and marble floors, and limestone fences.

The Ritz-Carlton, Bali was named by *Condé Nast Traveler* as one of the 'Top Five Asian Resorts'; and *Travel + Leisure* ranked it among the five 'Best Resort Spas Abroad.'

Client:	P.T. Karang Mas Sejahtera
Site Size:	173 acres
Project Size:	322 guestrooms, including 16 suites and 36 villas
Amenities:	6,400-square-foot ballroom and 13,000 square feet of meeting space; open-air dinner theater; two-tiered, fresh water swimming pool; 11,000-gallon outdoor saltwater aquarium; whirlpool; three tennis courts; 18-hole putting course; fitness center; 'Hidden Bali' culture tours; seven restaurants and lounges

The Ritz-Carlton, Bali

Jimbaran, Bali, Indonesia

Alatas Island Resort

Thessaly, Alatas Island, Greece

The resort is developed as a series of three villages set into the landscape of a rugged, 2-square-mile island.

This master-planned and fully integrated resort is being developed on an island in central Greece that is characterized by rock cliffs, steep slopes leading to vantage points, and a relative lack of flat terrain. Mature olive trees cover the majority of the island. A substantial portion of the island will be retained for open space and recreation.

The design concept calls for three major, interwoven components. The Harbor Village welcomes guests at a reception pavilion adjacent to a waterfront promenade lined by outdoor *tavernas*. Overlooking the harbor is a town center and the village residences. Located along hillside paths are a reception plaza, a conference center, and two-story residential villas. The development is sited to provide unobstructed views of the harbor and sea, together with amenities such as swimming pools and terraces throughout.

The Hillside Village features an open-air reception pavilion and residential villas with landscaped terraces. Located at the coastal edge of the village are two beaches and pool terraces.

The Spa Village features a spa and wellness center situated on a rocky outcropping on the hillside overlooking the gulf. Individual private bungalows provide guests with generous outdoor rooms and terraces with private plunge pools. Presidential villas offer even more seclusion.

Client:	The United Five Development Company Ltd.
Site Size:	1,359 acres
Project Size:	500 guestrooms
Amenities:	Spa and wellness facilities; meeting and conference facilities; educational spaces; retail; recreation; entertainment; dining

Borneo Resort Karambunai

Kota Kinabalu, Sabah, Malaysia

The concept for this master-planned resort is that of a traditional stilt village constructed of authentic materials, floating over Teluk Lagau.

The complex is envisioned as a living museum, offering guests a first-hand opportunity to experience Borneo and its unique heritage. Hotels on the site are designed thematically to fit not only the local culture but also the natural environment, which consists of jungles, mangroves, wetlands, beaches, and reefs.

The water village is the nexus of the entire Borneo Resort Karambunai, providing a mix of retail, dining, entertainment, transportation, and cultural offerings including the Tamu Gathering Place; 'Above Borneo' Skytram and Natural History Museum; Craft and Cultural Center; the Head Man's Hut; Water Stage; Angry Dragon spectacle; and Water Sports Center.

Water taxis transport guests to other points in the resort, including the Karambunai Water Park, which features rides and attractions based on themes derived from ancient lore, including a Malaysian Cave Cruise; Head Hunters' Village; Magical Music Pagoda; 'Wreck of Karambunai' Wave Pool; Misty Swamp Paddle Boats; Lazy River Ride; waterfall, and hot-air balloon rides.

Client:	Karambunai Resorts Sdn. Bhd.
Site Size:	3,600 acres
Project Size:	1,500 guestrooms
Amenities:	Water village; water sports center; living museum; water park; skytram; aquaculture farm; golf courses; residential and hotel accommodations

Aphrodite Hills,
Aphrodite Inter-Continental Resort

Pathos, Cyprus

The Aphrodite Inter-Continental Resort Hotel is one of the key elements of a master-planned development that is the first integrated resort community in Cyprus.

The Aphrodite Hills master plan is a fully integrated development, designed to include an international five-star hotel; an 18-hole golf course with a clubhouse and golf inn; 418 luxury villas; a retail center; a tennis academy and health spa; a tourist village; a cluster development; and timeshare units.

The Aphrodite Inter-Continental Resort Hotel represents the unique opportunity to create a premier destination on the west coast of Cyprus. The promontory location features nearby archaeological sites from the Greek, Roman, and early Christian eras, as well as the legendary Aphrodite's Rock, birthplace of the goddess of love.

The hotel is conceptualized as a retail village, with guestroom clusters that cascade down the site to create a hillside street experience. With the elegance and ambiance of a country manor home, the warmth of a stone farmhouse, and the use of other natural materials, the hotel becomes part of the topography. The retail center is the principal activity node, with shopping, dining, and entertainment options linked to a nearby amphitheater.

Client:	Lanitis Development Limited
Site Size:	578 acres
Project Size:	290 guestrooms, including 45 suites; 418 villas
Amenities:	Business center; six restaurants; health club; indoor and outdoor pools; international-grade tennis facilities; tennis academy; golf clubhouse and lodge; 18-hole championship golf course; spa; vacation ownership villas; village center

Taba Hotel Sofitel

Gulf of Aqaba, Taba, Egypt

Organized along interior courtyards and streets,
accommodations are designed to evoke a relaxed
village character in this desert environment.

This project forms part of a larger development that includes four- and five-star hotels, serviced apartments, private villas, and commercial facilities. All accommodations occupy prominent locations on the gently sloping site in order to take advantage of views of the sea, adjacent park, and Taba Mountains.

The architectural design of the hotel evokes memories of an ancient settlement, with antiquities and ruins punctuating the landscape. In response to the desert's hot summers and cold winters, the structures have thick walls and deep shadows defined by domes, vaults, and arches, as well as decorative grill work, geometric air inlets, and louvered shutters. The design takes full advantage of the indigenous masonry construction techniques and uses bricks made on site.

The guestroom villages are arranged as informal street courtyards of two to three stories built on and around 'ancient' ruins. The overall effect is a serene sense of calm in an environment that has a timeless quality.

Client:	Mansour & El-Maghraby Invest Co. Ltd.
Site Size:	40 acres
Project Size:	350 hotel guestrooms; 100 serviced apartments; 18 villas; 10 guest villas
Amenities:	Dive center; tennis and pool pavilions; landscaped pools and pool bar; four restaurants and lounges; health spa; amphitheater; retail; function pavilions

Urban Resorts

Enhancing the Guest Experience by Design
by Isadore Sharp

The French aviator and author Antoine de Saint-Exupery once wrote, 'In anything at all, perfection is finally attained not when there is no longer anything to add, but when there is no longer anything to take away.' To the hospitality industry, this means every feature of a hotel or resort must enhance the travel experience in a meaningful way. There is no room to waste.

Each design element incorporated into a new hotel or resort building, or retrofitted into an existing one, must be not only pleasing to the eye and other senses, but must also have a real function. It must serve to maximize the guest's ability to work when traveling on business and to relax when traveling for pleasure.

We are just as interested in providing well-designed business centers for the executive on the road as we are in creating fully equipped fitness centers for the vacationer or the business traveler who needs to unwind. Four Seasons guests have come to see our spas—many right in the heart of busy urban centers—as part of their overall hospitality experience.

We at Four Seasons Hotels and Resorts believe that luxury travel today is about comfort, functionality, and personalized, unobtrusive service that anticipates guests' needs. We understand the importance of all the invisible elements of success, such as the highest quality bedding to ensure a good night's sleep and ideal lighting for work and for rest.

That's why we oversee every stage of the design and construction of every hotel and resort we have developed. We choose architects and designers like WATG to create hotels that are showpieces of outstanding quality. All Four Seasons Hotels and Resorts are built to retain their appeal, not for five, 10 or 20 years, but at the very least, for the next half-century.

Isadore Sharp is chairman and chief executive officer of Four Seasons Hotels and Resorts.

Four Seasons Hotel Tokyo at Chinzan-so
Tokyo, Japan
Photography: Robert Miller

Four Seasons Hotel Tokyo at Chinzan-so

Tokyo, Japan

The architectural design of this hotel on the park marries
Eastern and Western traditions.

The design focus for this Four Seasons hotel is a 17-acre park in metropolitan Tokyo—specifically, the park's historic and honored Japanese gardens, which are a favored setting for wedding ceremonies. The hotel was designed to meet the client's wishes for unrivaled elegance and an atmosphere of serenity in the midst of a frenetic city.

Due to the limited 3-acre footprint, the design takes a vertical approach, with a 13-story tower. Portions of the hotel's interior design have a distinctly Japanese flavor, while the exterior features a contemporary treatment with its angularity and huge expanses of glass. The hotel's suites are furnished in either a Western or Japanese style. Many public areas and guestrooms open to the gardens.

Designed to be a haven from stress, the conservatory-like spa features a luxurious *onsen* bath, with natural mineral water from the famous Itoh hot springs. A dramatic enclosed pool has a barrel vault roof, which opens to let in natural light and air.

Chosen by readers of *Travel + Leisure* magazine as one of the 'Best Hotels in Asia,' Four Seasons Hotel Tokyo at Chinzan-so is known as *the place* for weddings and other special occasions.

Client:	Fujita Tourist Enterprises Co., Ltd.
Site Size:	17 acres
Project Size:	283 guestrooms, including 50 suites
Amenities:	100-seat amphitheater; business center; health spa; shops and gallery; wedding facilities; 26,000 square feet of banqueting and meeting rooms including 16 conference rooms; four ethnic restaurants

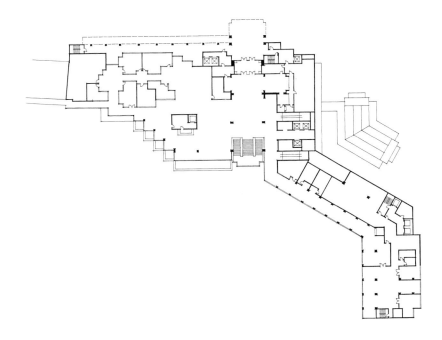

Four Seasons Hotel Tokyo at Chinzan-so

Claridge's

London, England, UK

The goal was to equip Claridge's with state-of-the-art, 21st century conveniences while preserving the charm and detailing of this 100-year-old Grade II historic landmark—all while keeping it open.

Immense care was taken to ensure that Claridge's style was preserved, with the unobtrusive introduction of highly sophisticated technology. Restoration of period details was accomplished with the support of English Heritage, and an electronic record on CD-ROM was created of the building and its contents.

As both architect and lead consultant, WATG was responsible for the smooth integration of a large design team, including six different interior design firms working on separate aspects of the project. Though there was a common design principle, all of the rooms were different in layout, furnishing, and finish.

A total remodeling of the hotel's sixth and seventh floors (previously maids' chambers) provided two penthouse suites, deluxe double rooms, a conference suite of private meeting and banqueting rooms, and a health fitness suite. New air conditioning was provided throughout the hotel; two high-speed lifts were added; all bathrooms were upgraded; and the basement area was designed for staff functions. As part of the refurbishment, the latest in-room communications technology was discreetly installed.

The £42 million (US$70 million) refurbishment improved sales by 38 percent and operating profits by 99 percent in the year following Claridge's renovation.

Claridge's is the recipient of numerous awards including: 'Top 100 Hotels in the World' (*Condé Nast Traveler*); 'World's Best Hotels' (*Institutional Investor* Annual Hotel Survey); 'Top 20 Foreign City Hotels' (*Andrew Harper's Hideaway Report*); 'Best Hotels in Europe' (*Travel + Leisure* magazine); and the 'Best Hotel in London' (*Hemispheres* magazine).

Client:	The Savoy Group
Site Size:	One city block
Project Size:	197 guestrooms and suites; two penthouse apartments
Amenities:	Meeting space; Olympus Health and Fitness Suite; restaurant and Claridge's bar

Mandarin Oriental, Kuala Lumpur

Kuala Lumpur, Malaysia

Designed as an urban resort on the park, the Mandarin Oriental, Kuala Lumpur thrives in a glutted market by attracting international visitors and residents alike.

Located in the heart of the city, adjacent to the Petronas Twin Towers and fronting a 50-acre park, this 32-story hotel was designed to uphold international standards and, at the same time, reflect traditional Malaysian influences. Materials (such as granite and wood) from the region were used extensively, along with Malaysian-inspired details and artwork.

With the largest ballroom in the city and conference/banqueting facilities for 3,000 people, the hotel attracts conventions, trade shows, business meetings, and large social functions. Each of the hotel's five restaurants has a distinctive theme and cuisine appealing to both guests and residents. A uniquely designed edgeless outdoor swimming pool is part of the 15,000-square-foot Mandarin

Oriental Vitality Club on the fourth level.

Of the 643 luxuriously appointed guestrooms, 184 of them are upgraded with even higher levels of service; and 51 executive apartments are available for extended stays. The Mandarin Oriental is a huge success operationally, boasting market leadership in both occupancy and revenue per available room.

Client:	ASAS Klasik Sdn. Bhd.
Site Size:	2 acres
Project Size:	643 guestrooms, 40 suites, and 51 executive apartments
Amenities:	Grand Ballroom (seating 2,000) plus Diamond Ballroom and 15 meeting/ function rooms; 15,000-square-foot fitness facility and spa; five restaurants; edgeless outdoor pool; two tennis courts

Four Seasons Hotel Mexico, D.F.

Mexico City, Mexico

In the midst of the world's largest city, on one of the world's busiest boulevards, the Four Seasons Hotel Mexico, D.F. is a secluded retreat that evokes historic traditions.

The design of this hotel does not attempt to mirror its immediate urban surroundings. Rather, it respects the traditions of European-inspired Mexican architecture and is derived from a blending of Spanish Colonial and historic French influences.

One element that contributes to the private feeling of the hotel is a low, coffered, formal carriage entrance. The entry, with its stone paving, glass lanterns, and mullioned doors opens into the lobby, which in turn opens into a serene central landscaped courtyard and surrounding colonnade.

The large courtyard serves as the hotel's focal point for dining and meetings and also provides natural light, gardens, and the sounds and sights of a fountain. While the inner courtyard and exterior façade borrow from Mexico's long heritage of Spanish Colonial architecture, the historic French influence emerges in significant decorative elements such as the wrought-iron scrollwork of banisters and the high, arched windows.

The Four Seasons Hotel has become Mexico City's most popular and successful business hotel. Readers of *Travel + Leisure* magazine chose it as the third 'Best Hotel in Mexico, Central, and South America.'

Client:	Proparmex S.A. de C.V.
Site Size:	1.75 acres
Project Size:	240 guestrooms including 40 suites
Amenities:	Indoor-outdoor restaurant; café; private business center; health club; rooftop pool area; 13,000 square feet of meeting space, banquet and conference facilities

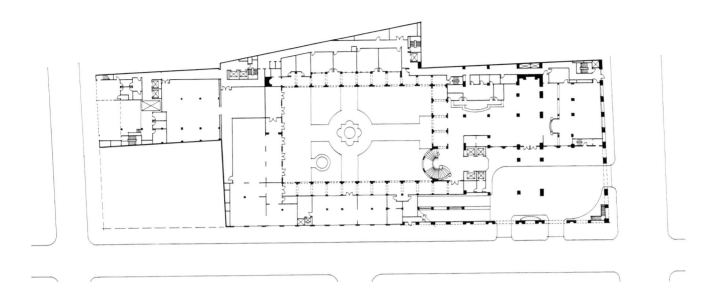

Mexico City, Mexico

Hyatt Regency Waikiki Resort & Spa

Honolulu, Oahu, Hawaii, USA

At the center of the Hyatt Regency Waikiki Resort & Spa
is the Great Hall atrium with three-story waterfalls,
exotic birds, and lush tropical foliage.

In choosing an octagonal twin-tower configuration rather than a single, less costly room block, the architects decreased room count but increased the number of ocean-view rooms. The solution also preserves a wide-view corridor between the buildings, lessening environmental impact.

The landscaping design provides tropical ambiance and sound-masking devices while creating a sense of human-scale in the block-long, four-story atrium that connects the resort's two 40-story towers.

While the retail component was critical to the economic viability of this project, there was insufficient space at street level for the desired 80,000 square feet of retail shops. The solution was a three-story podium and a circulation pattern that sends hotel guests past shops at upper levels.

The resort's Na Ho'ola Spa (*Na Ho'ola* means 'many healers') is Waikiki's first full-service spa and provides its guests with a uniquely Hawaiian spa experience, both through its specialty treatments and its interior design, which incorporates Hawaiian artifacts and sense of place. Na Ho'ola's 19 treatment rooms, exercise area, jacuzzi, sauna, steam rooms, refreshment area, and water features are located on two levels overlooking Waikiki Beach.

Hyatt Regency Waikiki Resort & Spa has been awarded AAA's coveted Four Diamond rating for 23 consecutive years.

Client:	Hemmeter Development Corporation
Site Size:	One city block; 2 acres
Project Size:	Twin towers, 40 stories each; 1,230 guestrooms, including 78 suites
Amenities:	60 retail shops; 17,500 square feet of meeting and banqueting space; swimming pool; three-story open-air atrium; business center; five restaurants and two bars/lounges; 10,000-square-foot luxury spa

The Regent of Bangkok

Bangkok, Thailand

Modern in every respect but also uniquely Thai, The Regent of Bangkok is designed as a gracious and efficient residence in the heart of a busy city.

The goal was to create an elegant residential-style building, combining clean postmodern lines with traditional Thai features. Artists and artisans worked with local materials such as hand-woven silks, teak, *maka* wood, and marble to give the hotel a distinctive style. A traditional Thai blue-tiled roof contrasts starkly with a gleaming white façade of plastered concrete.

Two open-air atria flank the main building core, and guestrooms open onto either the seven-story Parichart Court or the eight-story Mouthathip Court. Greenery spills down from each floor and, along with waterfalls and lotus pools, recreates the feeling of the Thai countryside right in the middle of Bangkok.

A carefully blended selection of traditional Thai artworks and contemporary crafts enriches the classically restrained structure. The monumental lobby, one of Bangkok's most acclaimed meeting places, features an entire ceiling of six painted silk murals representing the Thai cosmos.

Readers of *Travel + Leisure* magazine chose The Regent of Bangkok as one of the 'Best Hotels in Asia.'

Client:	The Rajdamri Hotel Company
Site Size:	4.2 acres
Project Size:	367 guestrooms, including 37 suites
Amenities:	Four restaurants; ballroom; conference center; business center; retail arcade; swimming pool with cabanas; rooftop tennis court; sports and health club; medical suite; two open-air atria with courtyards; two squash courts; beauty/barber shop

Four Seasons Hotel Newport Beach

Newport Beach, California, USA

A major challenge in designing the Four Seasons Hotel Newport Beach was to create a resort environment on a tight urban site.

The architects angled a 19-story stepped-back tower to protect the views of nearby office buildings and homes and provide panoramic ocean views for 100 percent of the Four Seasons' guestrooms. The property still allows for a large outdoor pool, tennis courts, terraces, and park-like landscaping.

A cantilevered porte cochere gives guests an immediate sense of spaciousness. Several design features—the tower's chamfered edges, the softening effect of landscaped niches at each tower elevation, terraced balconies, the private driveway entry and spacious turn-around—contribute to the hotel's feeling of a secluded retreat.

Public spaces were designed to contribute to the hotel's operational efficiency, productivity, and profitability. While the Four Seasons Hotel Newport Beach primarily serves the business traveler and does a considerable amount of conference business, its lobby remains a warm, inviting area in which guests can relax, read, or spend a quiet moment. Due to its steady mix of business and leisure travelers, the hotel consistently places far ahead of comparable properties in revenues and profitability.

Readers of *Travel + Leisure* magazine ranked the Four Seasons Hotel Newport Beach as among the 'Best Hotels in the Continental United States and Canada.'

Client:	The Irvine Company
Site Size:	4.5 acres
Project Size:	285 guestrooms, including 93 suites
Amenities:	Health club; 3,000-square-foot pool; two tennis courts; 17,000 square feet of ballroom and meeting space; fitness club; business center; fine dining restaurant

Hotel Inter-Continental Jordan

Amman, Jordan

The architectural challenge was to bring the 50-year-old Inter-Continental Hotel building, which had been modified over the years, up-to-date with a fresh and exciting image.

The architects were asked to upgrade the existing Inter-Continental Hotel and expand its amenities in order to re-establish the hotel's position as one of the leading destinations in Amman. New facilities include a guest wing of 125 rooms with a meeting room level and a shopping arcade, plus a fitness/ health club, banquet structure, and an underground carpark for the hotel. Existing public areas, guestrooms, and back-of-house areas were upgraded, as were the overall architectural character, landscaping, and main entrance of the hotel. Work was phased for the least disruption to guests, as the hotel remained operational throughout the renovation.

Acknowledging the Jordanian architectural aesthetic, WATG chose to reclad the hotel's façade by interweaving and tying strips of

fiberglass with thin, stainless steel cables to create a curtain which allows views out, acts as a solar shade device, and distinguishes the existing building with a unique look.

Landscape was integrated as a design element at the new pool deck and dynamic entrance canopy. By incorporating many cultural elements and details into the architectural and interior design, the heritage of Jordan is honored, and the hotel's status in the Middle Eastern market is maintained.

Client:	Jordan Hotels & Tourism Co.
Site Size:	4 acres
Project Size:	478 guestrooms including 30 suites and 20 business rooms
Amenities:	Business center; InterFit health spa; indoor/outdoor pools; ballroom, banquet and exhibition facilities; five specialty restaurants

Shangri-La Hotel, Garden Wing

Singapore

A striking example of 'landscape as architecture,' the Shangri-La Garden Wing reinforces Singapore's identity as Asia's Garden City.

An addition to the existing Shangri-La property, the nine-story Garden Wing presents a strong sculptural character. Drawing inspiration from the barrel vault roof of the original building are rounded balconies that step back as the height increases, forming a basic A-frame.

The designers brought greenery into the heart of the building with a nine-story atrium garden (the first ever in Singapore) that features over 45,000 plants, including 110 varieties of palms, trees, ferns, and rows of red bougainvillea. The vast tropical atrium lobby focuses on a waterfall cascading from its source two stories above ground into a rock-bordered pool below. Single-loaded corridors face the open-air atrium, providing a breathtaking view of the sky above and the gardens below.

Landscape elements—foliage, waterfalls, bridges, and paths—provide the resort complex with a unifying ambiance, both inside and out.

Shangri-La Hotel, Singapore was chosen by readers of *Travel + Leisure* magazine as among the 'Best Hotels in Asia.'

Client:	Shangri-La Hotel
Site Size:	12 acres
Project Size:	165 guestrooms
Amenities:	Open atrium lobby with waterfalls; sauna rooms; squash and tennis courts

The Ritz-Carlton, Marina del Rey

Marina del Rey, California, USA

The Ritz-Carlton, Marina del Rey serves as the focal point for the main channel of the world's largest small crafts' harbor.

The hotel's guest tower, two-story public areas, and intensely landscaped gardens are designed to emphasize the marine setting and to provide easy access to the waterfront and surrounding recreation areas. The distinctive 14-story postmodern structure incorporates a standing-seam copper roof and high-relief classic cornices.

Due to the configuration of the site, which slopes towards the water, arrival is into a second floor lobby that displays a broad view of the marina. Public areas are directed towards the harbor and public promenade, while each of the guestrooms features a marina and/or ocean view and French doors opening to a private balcony.

Only 5 miles from Los Angeles International Airport, The Ritz-Carlton, Marina del Rey is a world apart, a luxurious dockside retreat with the finest amenities and resort-like setting that includes a formal English garden and a promenade with seaside views.

The hotel received a Planners' Choice Award from *Meeting News* for being one of the country's 'Top 21 Urban Hotels.'

Client:	The Ritz-Carlton Hotel Co.
Site Size:	5.6 acres
Project Size:	294 guestrooms and 12 suites
Amenities:	Swimming pool and whirlpool spa; two tennis courts; basketball court; four restaurants and lounges; pool café and bar; fitness and exercise center; 12,000 square feet of conference and ballroom space with a conference concierge; 15-slip dock for hotel guests

Grand Hyatt Amman

Amman, Jordan

The Grand Hyatt Amman was designed to set a brand
new standard for city center hotels throughout the region.

The site for the Grand Hyatt Amman is on
one of the city's main thoroughfares.
Bearing in mind the importance of the building
as a civic landmark and the desire to provide
insulation from the traffic, the architects created
an articulated double-loaded guestroom slab
enclosing a tiered courtyard open on two sides.

The hotel is designed to capture the rugged
stone aesthetic, reflecting not only the local
character of Amman but also the uniqueness
of Jordan within the Middle Eastern Arab world.
Local stone is used on the building in a range
of finishes to create differing textures; the
courtyard and roof terraces are paved with
traditional patterns and banding and softened
with plantings and water features. The
architects echo the image of the famed Petra
Rock as a vertical cleft above the entry lobby.

The 15-story building includes three public
levels with seven meeting rooms, three
boardrooms, and the city's largest ballroom
(9,731 square feet). The Club Olympus fitness
facility features a gymnasium with extensive
exercise equipment; an indoor lap pool;
saunas, steam rooms, and jacuzzis.

Client:	Amman Tourism Investment Co., Ltd.
Site Size:	2.3 acres
Project Size:	316 guestrooms and suites
Amenities:	Ballroom/meeting room complex; six restaurants and lounges; retail mezzanine; entertainment center/fun pub/food court; fitness center and spa area; indoor and outdoor swimming pools

Merchant Court Hotel, Singapore

Singapore

Developed as an urban resort, this hotel takes advantage of its setting along the Singapore River.

The building comprises a 12-story main structure flanked by two five-story arms stretching towards the riverfront. In keeping with the rich heritage and style of architecture in the area, pitched roofs with traditional unglazed tiles are used, forming parasol-type forms over the corner pavilions. Materials, such as concrete with white stucco and brick trim, reflect those used on traditional shop houses.

The U-shape plan of the hotel's podium wraps around a private oasis of recreation, with an outdoor bar and swimming pool, gymnasium, and health spa facilities.

Dynamic vistas of the prime inner city island site are maintained, including those from the swimming pool with its 'horizon edge'.

To create a lush tropical environment with a resort feeling, the architects designed open colonnades and wide overhanging eaves. Exotic plantings and landscaped gardens contribute to the ambiance of this urban resort.

Client:	Merchant Quay Ltd.
Site Size:	2.3 acres
Project Size:	476 guestrooms
Amenities:	Pool deck with free-form pool and poolside bars; conference facilities; landscaped gardens; spa facilities; coffee house

Chevron Renaissance

Surfers Paradise, Queensland, Australia

A new landmark rises from the former Chevron Hotel, as a public gathering place on an urban site designed with a resort atmosphere.

The 129,168-square-foot, two- and three-story retail village at the heart of this urban, residential resort community has been created to evoke the character of a seaside village streetscape, with a town square at its center.

Chevron Walk—the pedestrian village street—is designed as a leisurely place to wine, dine, shop and stroll in the open air under the protection of deep awnings.

The architecture could be called seaside tropical Mediterranean, with stucco walls washed in white and light pastels punctuated by colorful louvered awnings of canvas and glass. Curvilinear walkways and tropical landscaping, including palms and ornamental trees, reference the subtropic beachside community that is Surfers Paradise.

Three serviced apartment towers (42 stories each), with wave-like curvilinear balconies, are sited to take advantage of views. These buildings are oriented to maximize sunshine for the resort-style pool area and lush tropical landscaping, which are located on a recreation deck that sits atop the podium parking garage.

Client:	Raptis Group Ltd.
Site Size:	5 acres
Project Size:	129,168-square-foot retail village with 650 serviced apartments in three towers
Amenities:	Landscaped recreation area; health club; parking; office and retail space

Casino Resorts

The Ultimate Resort Experience
by Sol Kerzner

As the competition to attract the guest grows more intense every year, our role as resort developers is no longer as simple as providing elaborate services. It now entails providing visitors with unique experiences that stimulate their senses and surpass their imaginations—whether in the casino or out by the pool.

This new trend, triggered by our transition to an 'experience economy,' has spun the birth of 'branded environments'—resorts with distinct personalities and unrivaled design strategies that cater to the new customer's need for exciting and captivating vacation experiences.

The success and popularity of Sun International's resorts speak well for this. I can honestly say that visitors to Atlantis, Paradise Island, and The Palace of The Lost City in South Africa—or any other Sun property—are literally blown away by the imaginative design and the craftsmanship that goes into creating each resort.

Our resorts begin with a vision and a focus on distinctive and original design concepts, from which creative energy and attention to detail flow to every corner of the property.

From the ground up, we strive for perfection in the smallest details of structural, architectural, and interior design. We bring projects to life through careful execution, with the help of talented people like the folks at WATG. The end result is a completely integrated property that has a natural connection to the local environment, stands out amongst its competition, and offers unforgettable experiences!

Sol Kerzner is chairman of Sun International Hotels Ltd.

The Palace of The Lost City
Sun City, South Africa
Photography: Courtesy of Sun International

Atlantis, Paradise Island

Paradise Island, Bahamas

The design brings the legend of Atlantis to life in expansive and vivid detail, with themed retail and entertainment, casinos, marinas, and water features.

Sun International rejuvenated, reinvented and repositioned this property to become the biggest island resort in the world: it has a 100,000-square-foot entertainment center, which includes the largest casino in the Caribbean; it offers 2,300 guest accommodations plus 38 restaurants and lounges; it features 11 million gallons of water activities/attractions and more than 100,000 marine animals.

The resort is themed throughout, with images of the sea and elements of the legendary Atlantis civilization. With a 14-acre aquatic environment, water is integrated into every design detail and every resort experience. While guests are welcome to a quarter-mile river ride or 62-degree drop water slide, they need not get wet to enjoy the underground aquarium complex and other amenities.

A sky bridge, 16 stories above the ground, links the Royal Towers. With 1,202 guestrooms and suites, the two majestic towers offer a range of accommodations, including the premier 10-room Bridge Suite.

Following the multi-phase renovation and repositioning of Atlantis, the resort achieved a tripling of revenue per available room. Readers of *Travel + Leisure* magazine voted the resort one of the 'Best Hotels in the Caribbean, Bermuda, and the Bahamas.'

Client:	Sun International Hotels Ltd., Sun International Bahamas Ltd.
Site Size:	60 acres
Project Size:	2,300 guestrooms
Amenities:	38 restaurants and lounges; three swimming pools; 40 waterfalls; river ride, slides, caves; world's largest outdoor aquarium; 50,000-square-foot casino with natural light; retail venues; full-service spa; sports center; 63-slip marina; and, in Phase III, timeshare and residential villas

Atlantis, Paradise Island

Paradise Island, Bahamas

Atlantis, Paradise Island

Paradise Island, Bahamas

The Palace Tower at Caesars Palace

Las Vegas, Nevada, USA

Caesars Palace—the first themed hotel and casino in Las Vegas—is still distinguishing itself and delighting tourists.

At the centerpiece of Caesars' expansion and renovation is the 29-story Palace Tower, designed in the resort's trademark Roman architecture style, with exterior fluted columns and Corinthian capitals and pediments. Following the line of the Greco-Roman façade, 1,134 new guestrooms vary in size from 500 to 750 square feet, each with a sitting area and 9-foot ceilings to enhance the feeling of spaciousness. Additionally, the upper two floors of the tower house 30 luxury suites.

Two of the Tower's lower floors are devoted to 110,000 square feet of banquet and meeting facilities, reflecting an influx of high-end corporate travelers to the Las Vegas tourist market. A 30,000-square-foot ballroom with 21-foot ceilings accommodates technical support for headliner entertainment. The Tower's second floor includes a 22,000-square-foot full-service spa and fitness center.

The 4.5-acre 'Garden of the Gods' swimming complex includes three marble-lined swimming pools and two whirlpools; three tennis courts plus landscaped gardens; statuary; fountains; reception areas; and a new pool bar and pool snack bar. Guests also can enjoy the Tower's added 15,000 square feet of retail space, an additional 8,200 square feet of gaming area in the casino, and four new restaurants.

Readers of *Travel + Leisure* magazine ranked Caesars Palace as among the 'Best Hotels in the Continental United States and Canada.'

Client:	Caesars Palace, Inc.
Site Size:	86 acres
Project Size:	1,134 new guestrooms and suites
Amenities:	ballroom/meeting facilities; spa and fitness center; retail shops; casino; restaurants; swimming complex

Las Vegas, Nevada, USA

Regency Casino Thessaloniki

Thessaloniki, Greece

The Regency Casino Thessaloniki is a successful hybrid that blends the refined style associated with a European facility and the familiar flash and sounds of a typical American casino.

Two casinos—a large American-style casino with 89 gaming tables and 640 slot machines, as well as a smaller European-style VIP Club casino (*Sallé Privée*) with 15 high-roller tables and its own private entrance, dining room and bar—appeal to guests from Europe, the Middle East, and Africa. Additionally, the facility includes a 500-seat showroom; show lounge/bar; a café designed as a Greek courtyard; a specialty restaurant; business center; hospitality suite; 1,000-vehicle carpark; and state-of-the-art security system.

Architecturally, the environmentally sensitive design reflects the indigenous Macedonian style, featuring low-scale buildings with thick, hand-troweled stucco walls, red tile roofs, and wooden shutters, doors, and windows. Variety in building shapes and roof geometry creates an unusual mixture of building masses. Outdoor terraces, courtyards, and balconies offer guests views of the mountain scenery.

A domed circular entrance and fountain provide an elegant first impression, which is sustained in the Regency Casino Thessaloniki's classically designed lobby. A high-end approach also can be found in the private gaming salon, with marble floors bordering the room and gaming tables made from fine, polished woods.

Client:	Hellenic Casino Company; Hyatt International
Site Size:	19 acres
Project Size:	107,600-square-foot gaming center
Amenities:	500-seat showroom; restaurants; business center

Regency Casino Thessaloniki

Thessaloniki, Greece

The Palace of The Lost City

Sun City, South Africa

A fictional account of a mythical lost kingdom, newly rediscovered, became the design theme for a luxury hotel of unprecedented opulence and originality.

The architects set out to recreate an architecture that never really existed, mingling images drawn from the rich lore of southern Africa. To add to the challenge, the client wanted the project completed in less than 32 months from start of design to grand opening.

Surrounded by water and approached across an entrance bridge, the Palace, with its vast arches and domed towers, seems to rise from its surroundings. In every monumental feature and in every minute detail, the Palace is designed to replicate an ancient and mythical royal residence. Guestrooms open to a five-story space crowned by a skylit ceiling supported by structural stone columns and accented with simulated tusk mullions.

The legends, written by the architects, call for a palace of great magnitude, as illustrated by

an 85-foot-high lobby rotunda—conceived as the royal entrance chamber. The richness of detail throughout the Palace includes 15,000 pieces of precast custom-made ornamentation inspired by Africa's natural vegetation and wildlife. A constant sense of movement is captured in sculpted animal forms and in the lines of arches incised with native flora.

The Palace of The Lost City was deemed 'The Best Hotel in the World' by *Lodging Hospitality* magazine.

Client:	Sun International Hotels, Ltd.
Site Size:	68 acres
Project Size:	350 guestrooms; 21 suites
Amenities:	Six restaurants; Olympic-size pool; water adventure park; 17 acres of lakes, rivers, and jungles; two 18-hole Gary Player golf courses; casino gaming

The Palace of the Lost City

Sun City, South Africa

Sun City, South Africa

The Venetian Resort-Hotel-Casino

Las Vegas, Nevada, USA

Authenticity is the basis for fantasy in this Venice-themed resort hotel and casino located in the heart of the glittery Las Vegas strip.

Mirrored after Renaissance Venice, this resort offers exact replicas of famous Venetian landmarks such as the Doge's Palace, St Mark's Square, the Rialto Bridge, the Ca D'Oro, and the Campanile Tower. Architects worked with historians to recreate with authenticity the feeling of being transported to Venice, complete with hand-painted frescoes, canals, and gondolas (with singing gondoliers).

The Venetian is the first all-suites hotel on the Las Vegas strip; it is also the city's first convention hotel complex. All of the 700-square-foot suites feature marble foyers, mini-bars, oversized bathrooms; and most have sunken living rooms. They are designed to cater to the business traveler, with three two-line telephones, a combination fax-copier-printer, and safes large enough to hold laptop computers.

To build a replica of 15th century Venice in record time, architects used 21st century technology. Working with a very large team of consultants from different disciplines and locations, the architects established an Extranet-based project management system, that served as a repository for the project's documents and accelerated design and construction, in response to a very tight schedule.

Client:	Las Vegas Sands, Inc.
Site Size:	63 acres
Project Size:	3,036 suites on 35 floors
Amenities:	11-acre rooftop pool deck and Italian gardens; Canyon Ranch Spa; four-level performance center; Madame Tussaud's wax museum; 11 restaurants overseen by renowned chefs; 120,000-square-foot casino; 500,000-square-foot convention facility and ballroom (with a direct link to the attached 1,200,000-square-foot Sands Expo & Convention Center); 500,000-square-foot retail/entertainment experience designed as a Venetian streetscape

The Venetian Resort-Hotel-Casino

Las Vegas, Nevada, USA

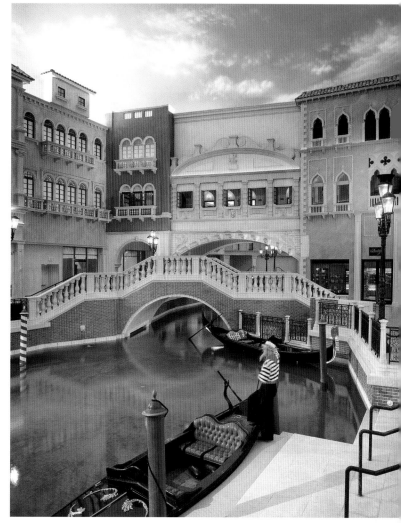

Las Vegas, Nevada, USA

Wild Horse Pass Resort

Sacaton, Arizona, USA

The Gila River Community, which represents the Pima and
Maricopa tribal cultures, wanted a resort that would
find its design roots in their history and cultures and also
respect the natural elements of the local environment.

Traditionally, the Gila River Indian culture
has been passed from generation to
generation orally from the stories of elders.
Through its architectural and interior design
services, WATG is assisting in developing an
authentic cultural program that can be shared
with visitors to the resort. The objective is to
tell the story of the proud Pima and Maricopa
tribal cultures without succumbing to the
fantasy or caricature that characterize many
contemporary themed resorts.

The Gila River environment will be recreated
after decades of hardship due to water
deprivation. The river will flow quietly
throughout the entire development, linking its
various components. The resort's architecture
will include some traditional forms such as the
vahtos, trellis-like shade-providing structures,
and a *humapek ke'* or gathering place.

The resort component at Gila River features
a heritage center, conference facilities, a large
pool, restaurants, retail shops, and a spa. Its
50 acres are part of a 2,000-acre development
that also includes an equestrian center, two
18-hole golf courses, a six-hole training
course, a lake, and a casino.

Client:	Gila River Indian Community
Site Size:	50 acres
Project Size:	474 guestrooms, 26 suites
Amenities:	Heritage center; conference facilities; pool; two restaurants; retail; spa/fitness center; 60,000 square feet of ballroom/banquet/meeting space; equestrian center; golf clubhouse and two 18-hole golf courses

Kangwon Casino Resort

Kohan, South Korea

Using a fictional narrative as its literary blueprint, WATG set out to create a mystical village nestled in the bowl of a mountainside, overlooking a valley and an emerald lake below.

Kangwon Casino Resort—with its steps, spires, dormers, and crystal-like central features—provides a dynamic backdrop for the village, which lies below. The hotel is reached in dramatic fashion through a tunnel, a cable car station, and ascending entry drive. It enjoys 360-degree views of the surrounding mountains, villages, lake, and valley.

To create a year-round village environment, the architects covered many of the streets and plazas—which host a variety of shops, restaurants, rides, fountains, and sculptures—with glass skylights.

The theme park is conceived as an integral part of the village and as a link between the hotel, casinos and condominiums. It consists of a 'Dry Park,' with rides and games, and a 'Wet Park,' with a wave pool and boat, flume, and river rides. The Kangwon Casino Resort includes the first casino in Korea for the domestic market and features a grand gaming room designed in the shape of a roulette wheel.

Client:	Kangwon Land, Inc.
Site Size:	51.9 acres
Project Size:	475 guestrooms, with two presidential suites (Phase 1); 450 guestrooms (Phase 2)
Amenities:	125,000-square-foot casino; theme park; 100 condominium units; 500-unit employee housing; health club/spa; pools; conference center and ballroom; six restaurants and bars; 400-seat amphitheater

Boutique Resorts

Small is Beautiful

by Marshall A. Calder

As noted British essayist Hilaire Belloc wrote in 1904, 'We wander for distraction, we travel for fulfillment.' Fulfillment involves exploring, discovering, and surrounding ourselves with all aspects of an environment in order to truly experience the culture and character of a destination. Key to this engaging travel experience is a visionary concept of what the experience will be, an innovative design to make it come to life, and the skillful execution of operational and service standards to make the experience memorable.

The small-scale luxury resort not only provides exceptional levels of personalized service but also affords guests the opportunity to become truly immersed in their chosen destination. Whether that destination is Mauritius, Malaysia, Tahiti, or Dubai, a rich and authentic sense of place enriches the total travel experience.

Boutique resorts offer guests a level of intimacy and service that combine with distinctive design to deliver a sense of luxurious escape—whether on a South Seas island or in the center of a busy city. Adrian Zecha was a pioneer in conceptualizing exactly this type of resort—one that seems to spring from its surroundings. That inspiration is manifested in his Amanresorts properties and in the work of WATG—both of which establish memorable settings through their unique architecture.

Thus the original vision, interpreted by talented designers, results not only in built environments of great beauty but also, ultimately, in the realization of a traveler's dreams.

*Marshall Calder is managing director of
The Leading Small Hotels of the World.*

Tanjong Jara Resort
Kuala, Terengganu, Malaysia
Photography: Courtesy of Tanjong Jara Resort

The Mansion at MGM Grand

Las Vegas, Nevada, USA

True to its original design intent, the Mansion represents the ideal 'centuries old' Tuscan villa.

Capturing the elegance and the exclusivity of an Italian palazzo, the Mansion caters to the invited guests of the MGM Grand Casino. Guests are chauffeured through a private gate that leads to a granite cobblestone-paved courtyard featuring a magnificent limestone fountain designed by the architects and hand carved by master craftsmen in Italy.

The design goal was to transport guests to another place, specifically, the Tuscan region of Italy. The architects incorporated design details, colors, finishes, and materials to provide guests with the ambiance and amenities one would expect to find in a mansion.

The grand structure includes 21 atrium villas and eight garden villas, which range in size from 2,600 to 13,000 square feet. Though there is architectural harmony throughout, every room is unique. Eleven of the villas have libraries and indoor pools, and all contain carved limestone mantles, dining rooms, and original artwork. The largest villas also include exercise and media rooms and additional bedrooms.

All of the exquisite atrium villas overlook the central atrium garden, which contains fountains and reflecting pools. The Great Hall, Grand Salon, spa, and private restaurant are surrounded by formal Italian gardens. Central to the gardens is the Grand Pool, complete with a sculptured marble obelisk.

To ensure the greatest level of privacy and security, the hotel is laid out so that guests can get to any room and to the casino without going outside. Despite outdoor temperatures in Nevada of well over 100 degrees, the 180-foot-square by 120-foot-high atrium is maintained at 72 degrees. The Mansion is closed to the public.

Client:	MGM Grand, Inc., MGM Grand Development, Inc.
Site Size:	5.35 acres
Project Size:	29 villas
Amenities:	Private entrance; Great Hall; Grand Salon; indoor and outdoor pools; spa; private restaurant; wine room; formal gardens; fountains and reflecting pools; handcrafted sculpture

Las Vegas, Nevada, USA

Hotel Bora Bora

Bora Bora, French Polynesia

The Tahitian-inspired architecture of Hotel Bora Bora captures the sense of place for which this tiny island is known worldwide.

Designed to be unobtrusive, the resort doesn't overwhelm its surroundings; it feels like a genuine Tahitian village with a South Seas atmosphere. In keeping with the use of indigenous materials and styles, the 80 thatched-roof bungalows (fares) form a village-like grouping of informal, open-air structures. Fifteen of these are suspended on stilts over the water.

Incorporating regional influences, the design of the Hotel Bora Bora affords great economy in both construction and operation. Use of readily available materials capitalizes on local resources and eliminates the need for air conditioning and other high-maintenance building elements.

The merging of modern comforts with Tahitian authenticity is apparent in the resort's high level of personal service and in the guest accommodations. The rooms are large (some, nearly 800 square feet); they feature high ceilings, separate living rooms, and private decks that lead directly to the water.

Recently renovated by Amanresorts, Hotel Bora Bora is the epitome of tranquility and, at the same time, rich in its recreational offerings. In survey after survey, it consistently ranks among the world's top ten tropical resorts. Readers of *Travel + Leisure* magazine ranked it among the 'Best Small Hotels in the World.'

Client:	Societé Hoteliére de Tahara'a, J.M. Long & Co., Inc.
Site Size:	16 acres
Project Size:	80 bungalows
Amenities:	Water recreation facilities; views of lagoon and beach from every room; tennis courts

Four Seasons Resort Punta Mita

Costos Banderas, Nayarit, Mexico

Four Seasons Resort Punta Mita—in its isolated setting
and its vernacular design—is tropical Mexico in every detail.

This new resort community was developed on Mexico's west coast, at the tip of one of the world's largest natural bays. Approached by a long, beautiful private roadway that skirts jungle and ocean views, the hotel is accessed through a cobblestone entryway and open courtyard that are reminiscent of the great haciendas on the original Spanish land grants.

All of the structures are low-rise including the main building, which features an open-sided traditional thatched *palapa*. Using materials that are indigenous to the locale—stucco for the walls, clay barrel tile for the roofs, and paving tile for the floors—the buildings appear as a series of elegant residences nestled into the hillside.

Mexican-style tile-roofed *casitas* of one to three stories house guestrooms and suites, each with an ocean view. Some of the guestrooms have their own private plunge pools. At the heart of the property is an outdoor terrace café with a Latin American menu and a large, free-form 'infinity' swimming pool that seemingly falls off into the ocean beyond.

A 100-unit vacation ownership community on the site has its own Resort Club Community Center. A visit to the Four Seasons Resort Punta Mita was chosen as 'one of the best trips for the 21st century' by *Travel + Leisure* magazine. *Condé Nast Traveler* magazine selected the resort as one of the world's best new hotels, citing its 'overriding feeling of unadulterated serenity.'

Client:	Inmobiliaria Dine, S.A. de C.V.; AEW Texas; AEW Mexico Co.
Site Size:	20 acres
Project Size:	100 guestrooms, including 21 suites
Amenities:	18-hole Jack Nicklaus championship golf course with eight ocean holes; advanced fitness center and full spa; tennis center; large, free-form pool; 3,700 square feet of meeting/function space; fine dining restaurant

Four Seasons Resort Punta Mita

Costos Banderas, Nayarit, Mexico

Le Saint Géran

Belle Mare, Mauritius

Extensive remodeling of this 25-year-old Grande Dame
of Mauritius has helped Le Saint Géran earn its title
as one of the leading hotels of the world.

On a private peninsula surrounded by pure white sand, Sun International's flagship property in Mauritius was remodeled to retain its feeling as a private sanctuary for guests. A 7,535-square-foot Givenchy Spa, one of only two in the world, is a new facility. The result is an atmosphere of refinement and serenity, with a deep blue lap pool at the center and a full range of body and beauty treatment rooms.

The resort features all kinds of outdoor recreation, from golf and tennis, scuba diving and deep-sea fishing, to basketball and water polo. Added to the private beachfront location, are 148 junior suites, 14 ocean suites, and a villa—all with colors and materials that contribute to an airy spaciousness and

elegance. A choice of dining venues includes Spoon des Îles, Paul & Virginie restaurant, and the open-air Le Terrasse. Each of the resort's bars—Pool Bar, Golf Bar, Casino Bar—is designed with distinct environments and selections.

Client:	Sun International Hotels, Ltd.
Site Size:	60 acres
Project Size:	148 junior suites, 14 ocean suites, villa
Amenities:	Givenchy Spa; fitness facility; hairdressing salon; nine-hole Gary Player golf course; golf academy; tennis club; sports center; boat house; gourmet restaurants; swimming pool; golf, swimming, and casino bars

Belle Mare, Mauritius

Tanjong Jara Resort

Kuala, Terengganu, Malaysia

Originally built in 1979, Tanjong Jara Resort was awarded one of the world's foremost prizes for architecture, the prestigious Aga Khan Award.

The basic design motif for the buildings of Tanjong Jara was found in the indigenous *istanas*, the elegantly crafted wooden palaces of Malaysian sultans. Climate-wise and cost-effective to build, the one- and two-story hardwood buildings (none taller than a coconut tree) were constructed 3 to 5 feet above the ground for purposes of security, flood protection, and air circulation. Rooftops are of locally made bisque tile; the underside of the tile was left exposed on the interior, allowing cooling breezes to circulate in guestrooms and warm air to escape through the roof.

As local hardwoods were abundant in the area, native craftspeople relearned traditional building skills to construct the resort almost exclusively of native woods. Decorative motifs employ authentic Malaysian arts and crafts, including wood carvings, woven mats, baskets, kites, and ceramics.

The Aga Khan Award jurors cited Tanjong Jara for the 'courage to search out and successfully adapt an otherwise disappearing traditional architecture and craft.'

Recently renovated by YTL Hotels & Properties to a deluxe international standard, the resort's original beauty and Malaysian feel have been preserved.

Client:	Malaysian Government Tourism Development Council (originally); now owned and operated by YTL Hotels & Properties
Site Size:	76 acres
Project Size:	100 cottage rooms
Amenities:	Conference center; swimming pool and lagoon; game rooms; three restaurants; tennis and squash courts; gymnasium and therapy center

Vacation Ownership/ Residential Resorts

Homes Away From Home

by Scott Burlingame and Richard L. Ragatz, PhD

Timesharing used to be sold as real estate. Then, as a vacation experience. But today, with the multitude of exchange possibilities available—including hotel stays, cruises, air travel, spas, and yachts—vacation ownership is becoming a product that appeals to buyers on the basis of leisure and lifestyle opportunities.

One of timesharing's strengths is that it can be modified to match consumer needs (that is, shorter, more frequent vacations; a variety of locations; and different kinds of vacation experiences, including bed and breakfast, beach resorts, boutique hotels, and dude ranches). With the hospitality and leisure company acquisitions of timesharing businesses in North America and Europe, it is no wonder Travel & Tourism Intelligence, an international research agency based in London, concludes, 'Timesharing is well positioned to become a major gateway to a host of travel and leisure services for the consumer.'

The high-end fractional interest concept—sold as a hassle-free and service-enhanced alternative to owning a second home—has been a particularly well-received product within the vacation ownership industry. Buyers purchase increments of weeks, ranging from a one-twelfth share with four weeks of annual use to a quarter share with three months of annual use.

This concept is characterized by large and high-quality resort homes. The challenge for the designer of residential and vacation ownership products is to provide owners with the desired level of hospitality and mix of amenities. Since many developers are now incorporating vacation ownership products into larger, mixed-use destination resorts, an additional challenge is to ensure the compatibility of uses and, at the same time, maximize economic return.

Scott Burlingame is editor and publisher of Vacation Ownership World *magazine. Richard Ragatz is executive vice president of RCI Consulting, specializing in resort timeshare industry research.*

Broken Top
Bend, Oregon, USA
Photography: Mike Houska

Hacienda del Mar Resort & Spa

Los Cabos, Mexico

Hacienda del Mar Resort & Spa is an all-inclusive vacation and golf resort community on a 1,800-acre master-planned resort with 2 miles of coastline.

Designed to recall the feeling of a colonial Mexican village, the development plan consists of four world-class hotels, two tennis centers, conference facilities, a beach club, and a town center, along with 3,400 single family residences, custom home sites, and condominiums overlooking several golf courses.

Spacious and bright, all 250 vacation ownership villas—ranging from studios to three-bedroom units—offer panoramic views, terraces, patios, balconies, and a seamless flow between indoors and out. Spread across 26 building blocks of heights ranging from two to five stories, the timeshare facilities include a dedicated reception building and a convenience store.

Connecting the various activities of the resort are cut stone pathways and fountains bordered with native greenery.

Client:	Quinta de Golfo de Cortez, S.A. de C.V.
Site Size:	26 acres
Project Size:	250 vacation ownership villas
Amenities:	5,000-square-foot conference center; 300-room hotel; six championship golf courses; tennis facility; pools; town center

The Bluffs at Mauna Kea

South Kohala Coast, Hawaii, Hawaii, USA

With its sweeping views of the Kohala coastline, this residential project was conceived by developers as a collection of stately Hawaiian homes suited to an indoor/outdoor lifestyle.

The project goal was to capitalize on a premium site by building distinctive second-home condominiums that would respect the local architectural traditions and island lifestyle. The Bluffs is set between the world-renowned Mauna Kea Beach Hotel and the Mauna Kea Prince Hotel, giving residents the use of resort amenities that include restaurants, shops, and lounges, as well as the golf course, tennis courts, pool, and beach facilities.

Due to the natural slope of the terrain, The Bluffs was designed to step with the grade, providing ocean views from every residence. Open areas take advantage of trade winds, and lush landscaping reflects the tropical environment. With the use of clay tile roofs,

heavy built-up plaster walls, and decorative inlay screens with teak and mahogany woodwork, the building materials have the feel of Territorial Hawaii.

Residents of this exclusive resort residential community choose from three different floor plans ranging from 4,000 square feet to 5,500 square feet in one-story configurations—all with the feeling and privacy of a single-family home. Each residence has its own pool and spa and detached two-car garage.

Client:	Mauna Kea Properties
Site Size:	45 acres
Project Size:	22 duplex home sites
Amenities:	Private pool; spa; guarded entry gate; golf club membership

Broken Top

Bend, Oregon, USA

Two key structures in this 500-acre residential resort—
the golf clubhouse and information center—set the
tone for the design of the entire community.

The client asked that the buildings be architecturally significant and that the clubhouse be versatile enough to function as a winter-sports clubhouse during snow season. With copper roofs, stone forms, and the prominent use of wood, Broken Top's design refines the mountain lodge-style architecture and complements the rugged beauty of its site.

The clubhouse appears to be rooted to a prominent boulder- and brush-covered plateau with 360-degree exposure to the lake, golf course, and forest land in the distance. The design is organized by the dramatic placement of two massive cross-axial walls constructed of stone, quarried, and cut on site.

The Great Room of the clubhouse is designed to serve as the community living room throughout the year. Exposed cedar trusses

support high ceilings, while expansive glass and a large terrace allow for panoramic views. The staircase has been created from natural boulders shaped like huge sculpted forms. Cedar stairs descend over and through the boulders, and one forms the base of a 30-foot-high fireplace.

Client:	Broken Top, Inc.
Site Size:	500 acres
Project Size:	27,000-square-foot clubhouse; 5,200-square-foot sales office/information center
Amenities:	18-hole championship golf course; pro shop; locker room; exercise room; swimming complex; public dining areas; members' grill; retreat for winter skiers

Bend, Oregon, USA

Emirates Hills Villa Estates

Dubai, United Arab Emirates

In the Emirates Hills Villas, a careful balance is struck between contemporary Western ideas of resort living and the desire of the local populace to honor traditional beliefs and practices.

Emirates Hills Villas belong to a community of luxury estates situated in the prestigious Emirates Hills Golf Resort on the outskirts of the capital city of Dubai. When completed, this large development project will cover more than 2,000 acres and accommodate an estimated 25,000 residents in a variety of unique residential neighborhoods.

Phase 1 consists of the main entry, gates, and guardhouses and the design of model villas that set the standard for future development. Four models, averaging 12,000 square feet, are situated on large, privately gated lots, each enjoying panoramic golf course views.

Every residence in the Emirates Hills Villas has two distinct zones of social interaction, based upon the traditional Islamic practice of separating the men's living areas (*majlis*) from the women's and children's living areas. Separate entrances are also provided so that men and women can circulate in complete privacy. Likewise, the gardens and terraces in the back serve both formal functions as well as casual family functions, with distinct outdoor spaces that can be separated and screened from each other.

It is the desire of the developers of this golf resort community that these villas not only set the standard for luxury living in Dubai and the region, but also introduce innovations of contemporary Western lifestyles (such as gourmet kitchens and casual, open, family spaces) to the local market.

Client:	EMAAR Properties PJSC
Site Size:	400 acres (Phase 1), 2,000 acres total
Project Size:	400 luxury lots, 3,000 residential units (phased development)
Amenities:	18-hole championship golf course designed by Montgomerie and Muirhead; golf clubhouse; golf academy; sales office; future schools, mosques, civic and commercial office buildings, par-three teaching course and another 18-hole golf course

Emirates Hills Villa Estates

Dubai, United Arab Emirates

Fiesta Americana Grand Los Cabos

Los Cabos, Mexico

On a unique site where the desert meets the Pacific Ocean,
Fiesta Americana Grand Los Cabos is a hillside oasis.

Rising 150 feet, the entrance lobby provides visitors with a breathtaking view over the hotel's hillside village and out to the seemingly endless Pacific Ocean.

From this main building, which houses the hotel's public spaces—lobby, meeting facilities, fitness center—an elevator tower leads down to a plaza and links private guestrooms with public spaces. Guestrooms are spread across several one- to four-story buildings arranged to work with the rugged topography. Luxurious suites have their own separate *casitas*.

Clay barrel-tile, low-pitch roofs have a light sand buff tone to fit with the desert setting. Further reinforcing the connection with the environment, natural rock from the site was used to create hand-fitted stone bases for the hotel's structures. Open colonnades and arches hearken back to colonial Mexican architecture and create a fluidity between indoor and outdoor spaces.

Echoing the design and layout of the Fiesta Americana Grand Los Cabos is a series of 233-vacation ownership units that complete the hilltown and also enjoy the shared amenities of the larger, master-planned development, which features a Jack Nicklaus-designed golf course that was ranked among the 'Top 100 Courses in the World' by *Golf* magazine.

Client:	Grupo Posadas S.A. de C.V.
Site Size:	27 acres
Project Size:	278 guestrooms and suites; 233 timeshare units
Amenities:	Fitness center and spa; four swimming pools; two tennis courts; 10,764-square-foot ballroom and meeting facilities; three restaurants and three bars; shopping arcade

Four Seasons Resort Club Aviara

Carlsbad, California, USA

Four Seasons' first venture into timeshare set
a new standard in the vacation ownership market.

The 240 villa units are arranged in three villages of buildings (two to six villa units in each building) around the Four Seasons Resort Aviara hotel. With the hotel, they share the white stucco and red tile roofs typical of Santa Barbara Mission architecture. Both are incorporated in the 1,000-acre Aviara residential development, with its golf course, tennis center, and wetlands preserve.

Villas have a generous 1,670 square feet of space, and every unit has its own outdoor entry. Each was designed with high-ceiling living rooms, fireplaces, kitchen, dining areas that seat six, two bedrooms, three bathrooms, laundry facilities, and three private balconies.

Each village is a community-within-a-community, with its own administration building, lounge, indoor recreational facilities,

swimming pool, poolside bar and grille, a shopette, and fitness center. Residents have ready access to the hotel's amenities, including its restaurants, shops, golf clubhouse, lobby bar, concierge services, and more.

Client:	Aviara Four Seasons Resort Club Associates Limited Partnership (affiliate of The Hillman Company)
Site Size:	51 acres (hotel, vacation ownership, golf clubhouse)
Project Size:	240 villa units
Amenities:	Villages have their own pools; poolside bars; exercise facilities; administration building; shopette; as well as use of the Arnold Palmer-designed 18-hole golf course and clubhouse; extensive tennis facilities; and five-star Four Seasons Resort hotel

Oak Valley Destination Resort

Kang-Won-Do, South Korea

Oak Valley Destination Resort is a self-contained, four-season destination for residents and visitors, on a rural site in close proximity to a national park, ski resort, and attractions of historic and cultural interest.

The Oak Valley Destination Resort consists of five major development zones that include three golf courses, multiple- and single-unit timeshare buildings, hotels, an alpine ski village, retail center, retirement community, and corporate training facility. The hillside site allows for long-range and golf course views throughout the development. The palette of building materials found throughout the complex includes natural stone, stucco, and slate-covered roofs.

The residential community is organized in a pattern similar to that of a small village. The village center, which is adjacent to three timeshare buildings, is situated on three levels that terrace into a sloping site. There, residents, guests, and visitors can enjoy restaurants, retail stores, and cinemas; a bowling alley, fitness center and indoor/outdoor pool; an entertainment plaza; two championship tennis courts; and an exhibition gallery.

Other timeshare units, as well as townhouses, are designed with unobstructed views of the golf fairways or the hillside. A distinctive 41,980-square-foot golf clubhouse is available to members and connects with a two-story reception building designed to welcome guests.

Client:	International Resort Corporation
Site Size:	3,900 acres
Project Size:	800 timeshare units
Amenities:	27-hole championship golf course by Robert Trent Jones II; reception building; golf clubhouse; fitness center; town square; bell tower

Golf an

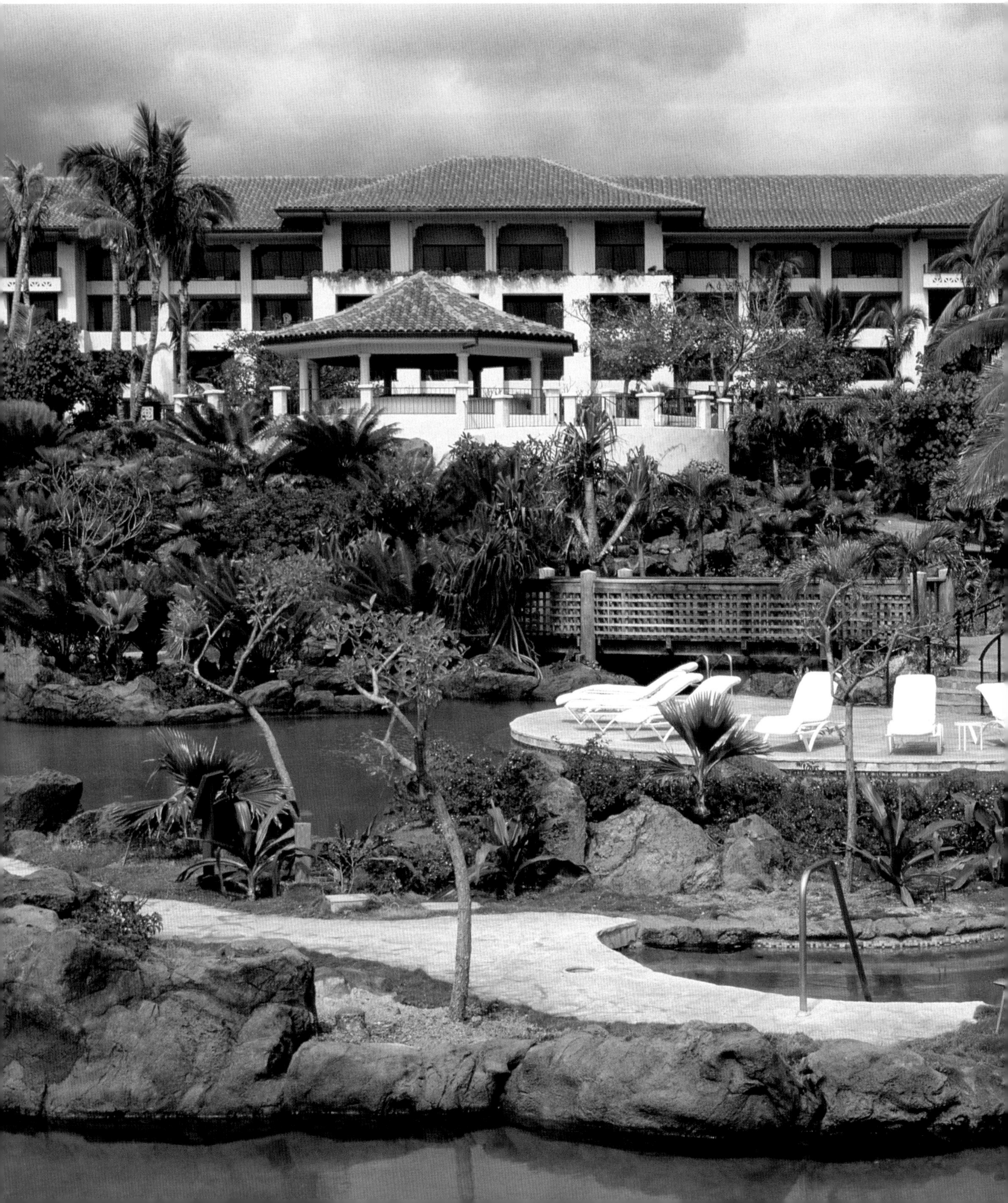

Golf and Spa Resorts

Oases of Tranquility

by Judy Singer

In the 1970s and 1980s, golf became an integral component of many resorts. In the 1990s, spas helped to redefine the resort experience. Through the first decade of 2000 and beyond, golf and spas will become even more important components of hotels, resorts, and residential communities.

People are in a constant state of 'rushing' to get things done. As a counterpoint, they need and want to relax more—both at home and when traveling. Today's busy individuals seem to be more in touch with the mind/body connection and therefore perceive spa and recreational activities not as an indulgence but as part of an ongoing effort toward overall well-being.

No longer the domain of only fanatical exercisers, spas appeal to the larger group of men and women for whom relaxation and health maintenance are important.

Health spas at home will raise the bar for resort-based spas, and both will become part of living healthy lives. Baby boomers who are attempting to manage the effects of aging will partake of future longevity and age management centers that offer Eastern and complementary medicine within the spa setting.

Spas will continue to be more holistic and will become more convenient to use, less intimidating, and, therefore, attractive to a broader range of people. The increase in electronic communication will only increase the need for personal connection. Years from now, spas may be one of the few places where people can find a high-touch and healing experience. And golf resorts will continue to be places where people can find open expanses of soul-soothing greenery.

WATG has known this all along. Their golf and spa resorts are oases of tranquility—special environments that beckon guests to visit and to return.

Judy Singer is president of Health Fitness Dynamics and The Spa Resource Group and chair of the International Society of Hospitality Consultants.

Hyatt Regency Kauai Resort & Spa
Poipu Beach, Kauai, Hawaii, USA
Photography: Milroy/McAleer

Mövenpick Resort & Spa Dead Sea

Dead Sea, Jordan

The Mövenpick Dead Sea resort draws on the history and culture of Jordan to create a destination with instant heritage.

The architects were challenged to create a one-of-a-kind property that would lure tourists from the more mature seaside destinations of Israel and Egypt. Mövenpick Resort & Spa Dead Sea is indeed unique, on several counts. It is the first international-standard, five-star resort in Jordan. At 1,320 feet below sea level, there is virtually no ultra-violet radiation to cause sunburn, making this location well suited to the wellness and spa markets.

Architects also took their cue from the native environment. Working with (instead of against) the sloping, boulder-strewn site, WATG anchored the resort with an ornate main building and grouping of guestrooms designed to recall the streets of old Jerusalem. The resort's village includes restaurants, shops, artisan workshops, and a courtyard typical of small Jordanian towns.

Throughout the collection of new 'old' buildings, designs were inspired by Arabic idioms and local materials, offering guests an authentic exposure to Jordan's rich heritage. In light of lengthy average stays of two to four weeks, the 232 guestrooms are spacious, and each is augmented by a shaded, private terrace.

The hotel's Sanctuary Zara Spa is one of the most sophisticated and extensive spa facilities in the Middle East, with more than 60 treatments and programs, including hydrotherapy pools with water from the Dead Sea. *Condé Nast Traveler* magazine, citing the resort as one of the best new destinations in the world, says it has 'brought new heights of luxury to the lowest spot on earth.'

Client:	Zara Investment (Holdings) Co. Ltd
Site Size:	16 acres
Project Size:	232 guestrooms, including 60 suites
Amenities:	Seven restaurants and lounges; function spaces (both indoor and outdoor); full-service spa; 500-seat amphitheater; three swimming pools; two tennis courts; artificial beach

Mövenpick Resort & Spa Dead Sea

Dead Sea, Jordan

Mövenpick Resort & Spa Dead Sea

Hyatt Regency La Manga

Cartagena, Murcia, Spain

This five-star resort hotel is actually the outgrowth of an existing, mid-market 47-room hotel designed as a 1970s modernist reinforced concrete structure.

Rather than tearing down the existing hotel, the architects stripped the building to its structural basics and transformed the central core into an enclosed Andalusian courtyard. The design brief called for transforming the outdated structure into a five-star hotel that would serve as the focal point of the resort and attract quality tourism to the region. Thirty of the original rooms were retained and enlarged, and two new guest wings were added. The long, low wings of the Hyatt Regency La Manga settle into the surrounding terrain and mirror in style and scale the neighboring village architecture.

To design a resort hotel that was both classic and contemporary, WATG architects drew from motifs found in historic Spanish villas of the early 18th century: arches, arcades, wrought iron railings, terra cotta roofs, and exposed terraces. The lobby's high, vaulted ceiling, stone floor, and white walls suggest the entry hall of an old villa, with contemporary interpretations evident in the selection of fixtures and furnishings.

The hotel now features spacious guestrooms, a large selection of dining facilities, and an impressive range of recreation options, all of which are available not only to hotel guests but also to residents of the resort's on-site apartments and villas.

Client:	Bovis Abroad Limited
Site Size:	1,400 acres
Project Size:	192 guestrooms, seven suites
Amenities:	Three 18-hole championship golf courses and golf academy; 18-court tennis center and tennis academy; 14 restaurants and lounges; gymnasium and spa; beach club; soccer field; crown green bowling; equestrian center; four swimming pools; banqueting facilities; library; jazz bar

Hyatt Regency La Manga

Cartagena, Murcia, Spain

The Ritz-Carlton, Kapalua

Kapalua, Maui, Hawaii, USA

The Ritz-Carlton, Kapalua was designed with attention to the small decorative details that reflect its Hawaii setting.

This resort was designed to give guests the feeling of intimacy inherent in a much smaller structure; the 550 guestrooms were spread among six buildings, each six stories in height and stepped down towards the coast. Public areas in the hotel were divided into three separate buildings, including a central main lobby building that opens out to an expansive view of the ocean, the 11,000-square-foot pool, and the richly landscaped hotel grounds. Each building was angled to maximize views.

The resort's architectural and interior design tries to balance the high-end style of a Ritz-Carlton with the more casual requirements of an island resort. The architects used large sliding glass panels to create an open-air feeling yet accommodate the windy climate of Kapalua.

Designed to respect the existing architectural style of the region, the simple building forms have distinctive gray-blue roofs with deep overhangs.

The pineapple theme is used as a decorative element on balcony railings, and Hawaiian floral patterns were cast into concrete panels.

With an ancient Hawaiian burial ground on site, The Ritz-Carlton, Kapalua established an in-house Hawaii Committee to help ensure ongoing support and preservation of Hawaiiana.

By readers of *Travel + Leisure* magazine, this hotel was chosen as 'Best Hotel in Hawaii' as well as the third 'Best Hotel in the World' and among the top of the list of 'Fifty Best Golf Resorts.'

Client:	Kaptel Associates
Site Size:	38.5 acres
Project Size:	548 guestrooms, including 58 suites
Amenities:	Three-tiered swimming pool with cascading waterfalls; 10 oceanfront tennis courts; over 45,000 square feet of banquet and meeting space; seven restaurants and lounges; three championship golf courses

Kapalua, Maui, Hawaii, USA

Hyatt Regency Coolum

Coolum Beach, Queensland, Australia

Set amidst rainforest and bushland, this project was conceived as a health management resort village.

In an effort to give the resort complex a residential feeling, the Hyatt Regency Coolum was designed on a decentralized village plan. A town square replaces the traditional hotel lobby, restaurants are served by a single commissary, and accommodations are spread out to encourage guests to walk or ride bicycles.

The golf clubhouse doubles as the resort's reception building. Guest quarters are grouped in three low-rise clusters set amongst the trees. Nine lounge buildings that function much like clubhouses invite guests to gather for breakfast and a variety of informal social activities throughout the day. The spaces between the clusters are as important as the buildings themselves.

The resort's architecture is inspired by elements of the Queensland style: lattices, trellises, and louvers provide shade and create interesting patterns and textures. Similarly, colors are borrowed from those seen in Coolum's rainforests, mountains, coastal marshes, and beaches.

Client:	Kumugai Gumi Pty. Ltd.
Site Size:	370 acres
Project Size:	330 units, including 174 villas and 156 suites
Amenities:	Robert Trent Jones II championship golf course; nine tennis courts; eight swimming pools; spa; salon; health management center; conference facilities; beach club; squash courts; creative arts center

Coolum Beach, Queensland, Australia

Four Seasons Resort Aviara

Carlsbad, California, USA

Four Seasons Resort Aviara was designed as
an integral part of a 1,000-acre, award-winning
master-planned resort and residential community.

Four Seasons Resort Aviara is built on a plateau overlooking the Pacific Ocean and the Batiquitos Lagoon, protected wetlands that are home to more than 130 species of birds (inspiring the name 'Aviara').

The world-class hotel, and the vacation ownership villas that surround it, are designed as an adaptation of Santa Barbara Mission architecture. Enormous windows frame outdoor spaces, and muted, natural colors and finishes create a luxurious but warm and inviting setting. A porte cochere and marble-floored promenade welcome visitors to the resort. Each of the deluxe guestrooms features an oversized bathroom and a landscaped terrace or balcony with stunning views of the lagoon, golf course, or ocean.

The award-winning golf course follows the natural topography of three valleys and adheres to ecological regulations imposed by the wildlife sanctuary. The residential resort of Aviara was named the nation's 'Best Master-Planned Community' by the National Association of Homebuilders.

Client:	Aviara Resort Associates Limited Partnership
Site Size:	51 acres (hotel, vacation ownership, golf clubhouse)
Project Size:	331 guestrooms, including 44 suites
Amenities:	Arnold Palmer-designed 18-hole golf course; driving range; 30,000-square-foot golf clubhouse; six tennis courts with tournament seating; fitness and spa center; large, free-form swimming pool; children's pool; 30,000 square feet of banquet/meeting rooms including 12,000-square-foot Grand Ballroom; five restaurants and lounges

Four Seasons Resort Aviara

Carlsbad, California, USA

The Orchid at Mauna Lani

Kohala Coast, Hawaii, USA

Taking full advantage of Hawaii's year-round hospitable climate,
The Orchid at Mauna Lani offers an indoor-outdoor experience
for guests in a luxurious but informal environment.

The use of residential scale and traditional European proportions, along with creative grading of the landscape, minimizes the visual impact of this hotel on its oceanfront site. The structure suits its landscape and appears smaller than its six stories.

A primary feature throughout the hotel is openness: guestrooms have balconies with six-foot overhangs; interior courtyards are open to the sky; and public spaces are oriented towards views of the Kohala Coast and the Pacific. In spaces away from dominant winds, the design takes advantage of ocean breezes and natural ventilation.

Double-pitch roofs, colored tiles, koa wood banisters, and regional motifs such as the large sculpted pineapples used as anchoring posts for stairwells, reflect the local heritage—a blend of European and native traditions.

On site, the design team created a swimming lagoon and white sand beach without disrupting the character of the lava and coral formations of the coastline. An ancient Hawaiian saltwater fishpond was preserved as a microclimate for marine life.

The Orchid at Mauna Lani was voted by readers of *Travel + Leisure* magazine as one of the 'Best Hotels in Hawaii.'

Client:	Colony Capital, Inc.; Colony Advisors, Inc. (renovation)
Site Size:	32 acres
Project Size:	542 guestrooms
Amenities:	White sand beach and protected ocean lagoon; 10,000-square-foot swimming pool; 11 tennis courts, including an exhibition court; two 18-hole golf courses by Nelson, Haworth & Wright; fitness center; three restaurants and three lounges; conference facilities

North Kohala Coast, Hawaii, USA

The Breakers

Palm Beach, Florida, USA

One hundred years ago, The Breakers set the standard for luxury resorts. After a multi-phase renovation and expansion program, the landmark property has reclaimed its famed status as a five-star, luxury beachfront resort.

The Italian Renaissance-style hotel has expanded with new facilities that include an Oceanfront Conference Center and a new Spa and Beach Club.

The conference center adds 25,000 square feet to the hotel's meeting facilities (for a total of 58,000 square feet) and includes a 15,000-square-foot ballroom, five new executive boardrooms, and 8,000 square feet of pre-function space.

The new 20,000-square-foot oceanfront Spa and Beach Club adds 17 new massage and treatment rooms and offers more than 50 different kinds of spa treatments. The complex also includes a 6,000-square-foot rooftop terrace, 25,000 square feet of oceanside outdoor function space, three swimming pools, and a tropical-themed restaurant that overlooks the ocean.

Completely self-contained, the 140-acre property offers two 18-hole golf courses, 10 tennis courts, and an on-site shopping complex. A new golf clubhouse, designed by WATG, is part of the ongoing renovation program. The addition of the spa and conference center is credited with increasing the entire resort's revenues by over 20 percent in the first year following its completion.

The Breakers was ranked by the readers of *Travel + Leisure* magazine as one of the 'Best Hotels in the Continental United States and Canada.'

Client:	Flagler System, Inc.
Site Size:	140 oceanfront acres
Project Size:	20,000-square-foot Spa and Beach Club; 25,000-square-foot conference center
Amenities:	Ten new oceanfront cabanas on private beach; three pools; full-service luxury spa; ballroom and 58,000 square feet of meeting space; seven restaurants; shopping boutiques; two 18-hole golf courses; 10 tennis courts

Hyatt Regency Kauai Resort & Spa

Poipu Beach, Kauai, Hawaii, USA

Nature's spectacular setting for the Hyatt Regency Kauai Resort & Spa, on 50 oceanfront acres, is its legacy and its challenge.

The designer and developer worked closely to take advantage of nature's scenic gifts while minimizing her wilder aspects, including brisk trade winds, unsafe surf, and salt-laden air.

The 600-room resort stretches out among lush gardens and lagoons in a series of attached four-story buildings radiating from a central pavilion. Double-pitch roofs of glazed terra cotta tile mirror the green hues of nearby mountains and verdant countryside.

A striking example of Hawaiian classic architecture, many of the resort's walls open to wide courts, gardens, and beautiful views. The flow of open spaces throughout the resort keeps its atmosphere informal and reflective of Hawaii's climate and culture.

Even with an architecture that is monumental, there is an elegance in the detailing—from koa wood cabinetry to exposed beams and floral motifs throughout—that echoes Plantation-era styling.

According to guest satisfaction surveys conducted by Gallup, the facilities at Hyatt Regency Kauai Resort & Spa are repeatedly rated the best among the more than 100 Hyatt hotels in the United States, Canada, and the Caribbean.

Client:	Ainako Development Corporation; Kawailoa Development
Site Size:	50 acres
Project Size:	600 guestrooms
Amenities:	25,000-square-foot health and fitness spa; four tennis courts; 18-hole Robert Trent Jones II championship golf course; five restaurants; five lounges; over 65,000 square feet of banquet and meeting facilities; 12,000 square feet of retail space

Hyatt Regency Kauai Resort & Spa

Poipu Beach, Kauai, Hawaii, USA

Hyatt Regency Kauai Resort & Spa

Poipu Beach, Kauai, Hawaii, USA

Palm Hills Golf Resort

Itoman City, Okinawa, Japan

As the initial project for an ambitious master-planned destination, Palm Hills Golf Resort is a showplace that embraces Western design and spotlights Japanese cultural traditions.

Palm Hills Golf Resort embodies the owner's mandate for an impressive Mediterranean-inspired architecture that accommodates uniquely Japanese conventions. The men's *furo* (soaking bath), for example, combines an opulent rendition of Japanese bathing customs and Western innovation.

In deference to Okinawa's cyclone susceptibility, finials atop a large atrium hold lightening rods, an anchorage system around glass areas supports protective panels used during threatening weather, and each roof tile is mortar-set. Broken roof forms give the building a residential scale.

The roof soars high above the atrium terrace, creating the opportunity for a garden-themed mezzanine level. In the elaborate VIP lounge, the design theme is expressed in arches and French doors, windows with stepped relief, and small, subtle downlights. An elaborate suite was designed for the owner, whose personal art collection is exhibited throughout the clubhouse and spa.

Client:	Takakura Corporation
Site Size:	12 acres
Project Size:	135,000 square feet of golf and spa
Amenities:	70-foot-high atrium with grand stair; four restaurants; VIP lounge; locker rooms and baths of both Japanese and Western style; notable art collection; interior and exterior gardens and water features; 18-hole Ronald Fream Design Group championship course

Four Seasons Resort Maui at Wailea

Wailea, Maui, Hawaii, USA

Although of palatial style and proportion, the Four Seasons Resort Maui at Wailea was designed to be in full harmony with its tropical setting and climate.

The client requested a 300- to 400-room hotel, all entry and public areas near the water, and ocean views from a majority of guestrooms. The U-shape of the building, a central courtyard facing the water, and guestrooms placed at a 45-degree angle to corridors give 85 percent of the accommodations an ocean view. Colonnades support deep eaves and give shelter to open-air, oceanfront public spaces.

Throughout the hotel, the architects use design elements to take advantage of, and enhance, the building's tropical setting: cross ventilation; sun-protected and breeze-cooled open spaces; natural lighting; the blurring of boundaries between indoors and outdoors; focus on water for sight, sound and feel; and the use of lush, exotic plant materials.

Elevator foyers in guestroom wings have natural light and ocean and/or garden views; so too with conference and banquet rooms.

Coffered ceilings, columned passages, rich interior appointments, and cascading fountains contribute to the building's palatial feel.

The Four Seasons Resort Maui at Wailea was named by readers of *Travel + Leisure* magazine as among the top 20 'Best Hotels in the World' and among the top five 'Best Hotels in Hawaii.'

Client:	Wailea Beach Palace Company, (TSA Development Co. Ltd.)
Site Size:	15 oceanfront acres
Project Size:	380 guestrooms, including 75 suites
Amenities:	Retail shops; 24,000 square feet of meeting and function space; dining options indoors and out; library; children's playroom; fitness center with spa services; numerous water features and gardens; two tennis courts

Four Seasons Resort Maui at Wailea

Wailea, Maui, Hawaii, USA

The Ritz-Carlton, Huntington Hotel & Spa

Pasadena, California, USA

Renovation of this large, historic hotel required a mixture
of new construction, replication, and restoration.

In a two-year, fast-track program, WATG set out to transform the 87-year-old Huntington Hotel from an outmoded, structurally unsound facility to a luxury resort hotel equipped to meet every modern demand. The architects went to great lengths to preserve the hotel's heritage, rebuilding and recycling wherever possible.

In replicating the hotel's tower, all of the building's spaces, including many that had been unconventionally narrow, were reconfigured for improved flexibility and function. An entry portal, recalling the original archway used for horse carriages, was reproduced to create a new porte cochere and lobby.

The elaborate, vaulted ceilings of the historic Georgian Room were repaired and reinforced, and the former ballroom was transformed into an elegant dining room. The carriage house was redesigned as retail and office space, while the old kitchen was converted to meeting rooms. Several cottages on the property were restored for guest use; one, an English-style 1930s bungalow, has become the hotel's health club.

Lauded as 'extraordinary to perfection' in a Zagat readers' poll, The Ritz-Carlton, Huntington Hotel & Spa in Pasadena was also cited by its current owners as 'the best performing real estate investment' in their entire portfolio. *Condé Nast Traveler* named it as number three in the list of 'Top North American Hotels,' and *Fitness* magazine ranked it number one of the 'Top 20 Spas in the Country.'

Client:	Huntington Hotel Partners
Site Size:	23 acres
Project Size:	392 guestrooms, including six cottages and 22 suites
Amenities:	First Olympic-size pool in California; three tennis courts; five restaurants and lounges; fitness center; 25,000 square feet of meeting facilities, including 12,000-square-foot Grand Ballroom, 4,500-square-foot Viennese Junior Ballroom and 8,500 square feet of additional meeting rooms

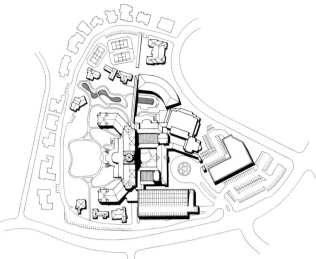

The Ritz-Carlton, Huntington Hotel & Spa

Hapuna Beach Prince Hotel

Kohala Coast, Big Island, Hawaii, USA

The architects, in designing with great sensitivity to the environment, took measures to protect the area's natural springs, which are the source of the name 'Hapuna.'

When Laurance Rockefeller built the Mauna Kea Beach Hotel on a lava field overlooking a beautiful white sand beach, he originally envisioned a resort with two hotels and a golf course. The Hapuna Beach Prince Hotel is the fulfillment of that dream.

The hotel's large, open-air lobby was designed to be cooled by Hawaii's gentle trade winds and to bring spectacular views and natural landscaping inside. Four low-rise structures overlook Hapuna Beach on two different levels; a feeling of cohesiveness is reinforced by multi-colored China slate that appears through the resort's lush gardens of tropical plants and trees.

Environmental considerations, including energy conservation and recycling, received great attention during the hotel's planning. The Hapuna Beach Golf Course has been nationally recognized for its environmental sensitivity, and several different species of native birds make their home there.

All of the guestrooms and suites face the ocean with breathtaking views from each room's private deck. An exclusive, 8,000-square-foot Hapuna Suite can be reached from its own driveway and porte cochere.

Readers of *Travel + Leisure* magazine chose Hapuna Beach Prince Hotel as among the 'Best Hotels/Resorts in Hawaii.'

Client:	Mauna Kea Properties, Inc.
Site Size:	32 oceanfront acres
Project Size:	350 guestrooms, including 36 suites
Amenities:	Five restaurants; two lounges; 21,000 square feet of conference and meeting space; spa and fitness center; freshwater swimming pool; championship 18-hole golf course designed by Arnold Palmer; tennis complex; retail shops

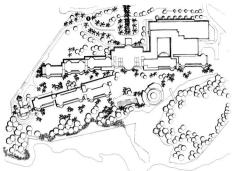

Le Meridien Nirwana Golf & Spa Resort

Tabanan, Bali, Indonesia

Cultural and site sensitivity were paramount in the design
of this property, within sight of the famed Tanah Lot Temple.

As Bali's first, fully-integrated resort development, Nirwana Bali Resort combines world-class golf and recreational facilities, exclusive residential villas and resort homes, as well as the five-star Le Meridien Nirwana Golf & Spa Resort.

Balinese water gardens are an integral part of the hotel entry experience; and a strong relationship is created between architecture, landscaping, water gardens and water features. The hotel is oriented to afford views of Tanah Lot Temple, rice terraces, and the sea. Designed on a village model, the hotel architecture features open-facing traditional Balinese-style one- and two-bedroom bungalows and medium-rise structures. Guests have the luxury of private pools, terraces, and courtyards; indoor and outdoor pavilions, and Balinese baths.

Within the heart of the resort, luxury villas and resort homes are set in clusters. All are designed and constructed in a traditional Balinese style and offer seven alternative choices of floor plans and views.

Client:	P.T. Bakrie Nirwana Resort
Site Size:	299 acres
Project Size:	278 guestrooms and over 700 residential units, including 380 resort homes, 157 luxury villas, 150 timeshare units, plus townhouses and executive homes
Amenities:	Seaside amphitheater; racquet sports center; clubhouse; 30,000-square-foot thalassotherapy spa; 18-hole Greg Norman championship golf course; seven restaurants; meeting, boardroom and ballroom space

The Conference Center & Spa at Le Meridien Limassol Spa & Resort

Limassol, Cyprus

The first of its kind, not only in Cyprus but in the Eastern Mediterranean, Le Meridien Limassol Spa & Resort was designed to set new standards in a new market.

The architectural goal of this project was to design a place that could be perceived immediately as Cypriot while at the same time blending with its landscape. The luxurious seafront spa is completely immersed in orange trees, olive trees, cypress trees, and other indigenous plants, as well as local aromatic herbs used as ground cover.

This oasis of relaxation includes four outdoor seawater pools—each with a different salinity content and temperature—a steam bath, saunas, whirlpools, plunge pools, and 20 treatment rooms. Created as a 'hotel within a hotel,' the spa has its own accommodations with 18 new rooms in the Royal Spa Wing, six cabanas with private jacuzzis, and four Royal Suites.

The sea is used to greatest advantage, not just for its views from every room, but as supplier of mineral salts, vitamins and chlorophyll, and other elements that are used as part of a long list of specialized therapies to promote relaxation and rejuvenation.

Client:	L'Union Nationale Tourism
Site Size:	32,292 square feet
Project Size:	53,820-square-foot conference center and spa
Amenities:	Four outdoor pools and three indoor pools (including the largest seawater pool on Cyprus); waterfalls and grottoes; accommodations of various configurations; 20 spa treatment rooms; 21 spa packages and medically certified staff

Thematic Resorts

Capitalizing on Fantasy

by Véronique Vienne

At the beginning of the twentieth century, while wealthy Europeans indulged in month-long water cures at resort spas, Americans seldom took time off to get away, even for health reasons. Back then, taking it easy was frowned upon.

Everything changed about a century ago, when trolley companies on the east coast created amusement parks at the end of their lines to boost their weekend business. Palisades Park, at the end of New Jersey's Bergen County Traction Company line, opened to the public in 1898— an early blueprint for many resorts to come.

Though much more imposing than their trolley-park ancestors, today's resort environments still attempt to attract customers to the end of the line. When guests get to their final destination, they want to feel like they've *arrived.* They want to put down their baggage and exhale.

Unlike the traditional hotel industry, which caters to travelers in transit, the resort business is all about keeping people in one location. Creating a sense of place—and selling it—is what resort development is all about. Developers leverage the uniqueness of their resort to enhance the value of the land around it. Some analysts even argue that hospitality design is a subset of the real estate business, not the tourist industry.

Resort architects have to be sensualists as much as builders—their most critical challenge is understanding what guests expect in terms of relaxation, escape, novelty, and enrichment.

WATG understands that theming is just another form of entertainment—the creation of a fantasy in which guests can immerse themselves. But beware: only in the hands of masters will the fantasy feel real.

Véronique Vienne writes for House & Garden *and* Architectural Record *and is the author of* The Art of Doing Nothing.

Disney's Grand Floridian Resort and Spa
Walt Disney World Resort, Lake Buena Vista, Florida, USA
Photography; ©Disney Enterprises, Inc.,
used with permission from Disney Enterprises, Inc.

Disneyland® Hotel at the DISNEYLAND® Paris Resort

Marne-la-Vallée, France

As the destination's flagship resort, Disneyland Hotel Paris incorporates the entry gates to the Magic Kingdom in its design—a first for any Disney theme park.

Designed as an elegant, turn-of-the-century Queen Anne Victorian mansion, the pastel-pink hotel—with its gingerbread, cupolas, chimneys, finials, and red-shingled roof—provides an enchanting fairytale ambiance. The luxury hotel is approached through the Fantasia Gardens, from which the face of Mickey Mouse on a clock tower beckons guests.

Conceived by Walt Disney Imagineering in collaboration with WATG, the hotel features a main building set high over the entry point to the theme park and two wings. Many of the hotel's guestrooms overlook the Magic Kingdom or Fantasia Gardens, and top-floor suites have outstanding views of Sleeping Beauty Castle. Decorated in pastel shades, the spacious guestrooms incorporate Disney images throughout, such as on the tiled frieze in suite bathrooms.

All suites are individually themed (for example, Cinderella Suite), and those on the hotel's top two floors have extra amenities—a private elevator, separate reception desk, and lounge—that distinguish the 50-room boutique hotel within a hotel called the Castle Club.

The British Travel Agents Association selected the five-star Disneyland Hotel Paris as the 'European Hotel of the Year.'

Client:	Euro Disney SCA
Site Size:	5,000-acre Disneyland Paris Resort
Project Size:	500 guestrooms and suites
Amenities:	Three restaurants; indoor heated swimming pool and pool house; fitness club; arcade/game room; Castle Club

Disney characters © Disney Enterprises, Inc.

Disney characters © Disney Enterprises, Inc.

Disney characters © Disney Enterprises, Inc.

Disney characters © Disney Enterprises, Inc.

Palace of the Golden Horses

Kuala Lumpur, Malaysia

Palace of the Golden Horses is the crown jewel
of the Mines Resort City, a 1,000-acre mixed-use
development with activities linked by water.

The hotel is designed around a series of courtyards and sun-protected open spaces, in keeping with the tropical climate. As the country's first themed resort hotel, the Palace of the Golden Horses is a contemporary reflection of the British Colonial-period Moorish design common to Malaysia. Many architectural details are based on 12 newly created legends scripted by the architects.

True to its name, the hotel is designed to be a palace in every respect. The architecture of the hotel is characterized by towers and domes that shape unique guestrooms and provide multiple observation points overlooking the lake and surrounding hills. The Grand Salon, the gemstone of the hotel complex, exudes the splendor of a bygone era.

Malaysian influence can be seen throughout the hotel in the use of local flora and fauna, traditional textiles, and historic architectural features. To further emphasize the natural attributes of Malaysia, the swimming pool is designed as an integral part of a botanical garden.

Client:	Country Heights Holdings Bhd.
Site Size:	13 acres
Project Size:	481 guestrooms, including 80 suites
Amenities:	Conference center with two ballrooms, 518-seat auditorium, boardroom, 20 meeting rooms; business center; eight specialty restaurants; landscaped pool; spa and fitness center

The Shilla, Cheju

Cheju Island, South Korea

Korea's very first resort hotel, The Shilla, Cheju
was designed—at the client's request—to provide a
California-style vacation experience for Korean guests.

The client's intent was to bring something exotic to local Korean guests: namely, Southern Californian Mediterranean-style architecture, with its stucco walls, arched windows and portals, terra cotta tile roofs, and reinforced concrete structure.

Behind the California Spanish style in Cheju is a hotel that easily accommodates Korean customs: public spaces and function areas are designed to comfortably hold traditionally large weddings. To create more intimately scaled spaces within the hotel's large lobby, the architects designed oversized, glass-screen tile-block dividing walls.

Arriving guests enter a central building which presides over ocean vistas and radiates to four guest wings, each with five stories.

The resort has been host to international conferences and high-level summits and praised by heads of state and dignitaries like Bill Clinton, Mikhail Gorbachev, and H.E. Jiang Zemin.

Client:	The Shilla Hotels & Resorts Company, (Samsung Group)
Site Size:	21 acres
Project Size:	429 guestrooms, including 12 Korean rooms and 38 suites
Amenities:	Three restaurants; three bars; seven banquet halls; casino; duty-free shop; fitness club; indoor/outdoor pool; six-lane bowling alley; 18-hole golf course

Disney's Grand Floridian Resort and Spa

Walt Disney World Resort, Lake Buena Vista, Florida, USA

Walt Disney Imagineering conceived the design concept for a spirited re-creation of turn-of-the-century Victorian architecture in a 900-room world-class resort hotel.

Faced with an existing monorail system that had to meld with the main building, the team designed a Victorian-style train station as the hotel entry and porte cochere. An arcaded bridge leads to the hotel's atrium lobby. The 85-foot-high ceiling of the five-story atrium lobby is crowned by domed skylights.

To create a comfortable atmosphere in an immense hotel, buildings are arranged village-style and limited to five stories. A wide, artificial white sand beach completes the scenario for this themed resort, where every detail was carefully thought out to create a seamless fantasy. For fire safety and long-term maintenance, fiberglass was used to replicate wood for most grillwork, brackets, and posts. Wherever guests might touch or observe surfaces at close range, such as stairways and banisters in the atrium lobby, wood is used.

Disney's Grand Floridian Resort and Spa was voted one of the three 'Best Resort Hotels in North America' by 20,000 travel agents. Readers of *Travel + Leisure* magazine ranked the property among the top 10 'Best Hotels in the Continental U.S. and Canada.'

Client:	Disney Development Company
Site Size:	40 acres
Project Size:	900 rooms
Amenities:	Monorail station; seven restaurants and lounges; health club; spa; 8,000-square-foot pool; two tennis courts; snack bar; arcade; child-care facility; marina; retail shops; convention facilities; wedding chapel

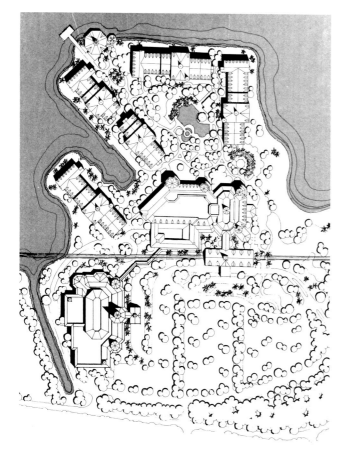

Lotte World Tokyo

Tokyo, Japan

The world's largest dome houses Lotte World Tokyo—the first themed urban entertainment center in Japan.

This large, mixed-use complex consists of an indoor entertainment park covered by a 290-meter (900-foot) dome, three hotels, an indoor snow slope, and themed retail streets, as well as movie theaters and food and beverage outfits.

Working closely with the client, the architects developed thematic concepts and created story lines in order to script memorable guest experiences.

There are five distinct zones within the domed environment—each with its own theme: adventure, romance, festivity, mystery, and fantasy. Architectural details are drawn from images of cultures from around the world.

Client:	Lotte World Ltd
Site Size:	47 acres
Project Size:	Three hotels, 750 guestrooms total
Amenities:	Indoor theme park and attractions; wedding chapel; banquet halls; movie theaters; retail facilities

Advance Bookings

Check into the Future

by Rowan Moore

Once upon a time, before humans landed on the moon, everyone knew what modern hotels looked like. They were big, none-too-charming offshoots of the international style in architecture. They were the architectural equivalent of the business suit. They gave no real pleasure.

The architects and designers at Wimberly Allison Tong & Goo have changed all that. They script experiences and then build them. Hotels such as Atlantis in the Bahamas and The Venetian in Las Vegas resemble small cities, within whose boundaries a tourist's every need or pleasure may be satisfied.

In the future, more people will go on holiday and they will spend more, which will drive hotels to find new locations and attention-seeking spectacles. Travelers will become ever more demanding, looking for experiences they can imagine no one else is having.

WATG is leading the way in creating out-of-this-world experiences—with projects on the boards that will take visitors below the surface of the sea and beyond our earth's atmosphere. Their notion is that a hotel need not be rooted in one place.

The airship WATG has dreamed up for *Condé Nast Traveller* embodies the moving hotel concept, making it into a millennial cruise ship, with the added attractions of skydiving and bungee jumping. Its futurism is combined with a dose of nostalgia for leisurely, luxurious Atlantic crossings.

Resorts of the future will be more than just places to stay. They will offer the experience of a lifetime.

Rowan Moore is the architecture critic of the London Evening Standard *and author of numerous books. This essay was excerpted from an article that first appeared in* Condé Nast Traveller.

Airship Hotel
Rendering: POD Productions

Airship Hotel

The journey itself is the experience aboard this luxurious floating hotel nicknamed 'The Airient Express.'

The entire structure is suspended below two helium balloons, affording guests not only constantly changing 360-degree vistas but also views to the landscape below (by means of glass floors). Public spaces—where guests can gather to learn, to converse, and to have fun—include the library, the map room, and the ballroom.

The 50 guestrooms form the spine of the airship and lead to the Plank, from which guests can bungee jump or skydive. Those who are less adventurous can simply enjoy the elegance and leisurely pace of this civilized form of travel.

Renderings: POD Productions

America World City Ship

Six thousand passengers can enjoy leisure travel, meetings, and conventions aboard this floating resort, which houses its own marina inside the hull.

Nearly a quarter of a mile long and almost 300 feet wide, the world's largest ship offers spacious guestrooms and suites in three hotel towers, with panoramic views that keep changing.

America World City is designed as a city-at-sea, with an array of restaurants and shops; nightclubs, theaters, and television studios; and spas, fitness facilities, and recreational activities. It also includes extensive meeting/exhibition space, an educational complex, and a science and technology concourse.

Renderings: Ted Lodigensky (top); Robert McCall (bottom)

Space Resort

Orbiting 200 miles above our planet, guests can experience a full range of weightless recreational activities and views that are out-of-this-world.

WATG's space resort incorporates, as its basic building module, recycled and retrofitted external tanks from future space shuttle launches.

The outer ring of the resort, housing the guestrooms, rotates slowly to create a quarter of Earth's gravity, enabling guests to enjoy the comfort of reclining on inflatable beds (rather than being zipped into sleeping bags that are attached to the wall with Velcro). Passengers are ferried to and from the resort by a new generation of reusable launch vehicles.

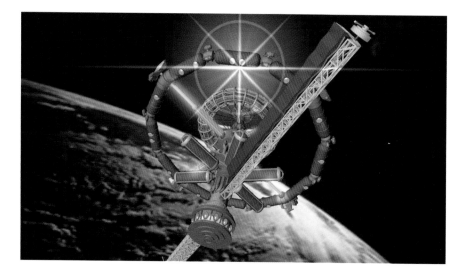

Constellation City

The city as an urban entertainment center becomes a resort destination for tourists and residents alike.

Constellations of activity centers—marina, theme park, aquarium, museums, casinos, hotels, retail, restaurants, and recreation—provide visitors with an entire array of entertainment experiences.

Undersea Hotel

Most of the visitors to this undersea hotel are of the marine variety. Human guests can stay in one of 80 rooms and be closely observed by their underwater neighbors.

The hotel, attached to shore by a long boardwalk, includes below-the-waterline guestrooms (with waterbeds, of course), a marine research laboratory, and an observatory. Above-sea-level facilities include a restaurant, wedding chapel, sunbathing decks, and docks for pleasure craft.

Geographical Index

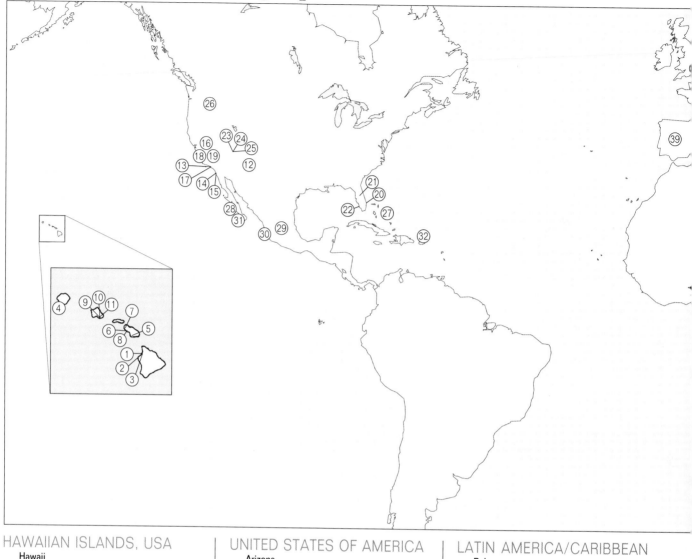

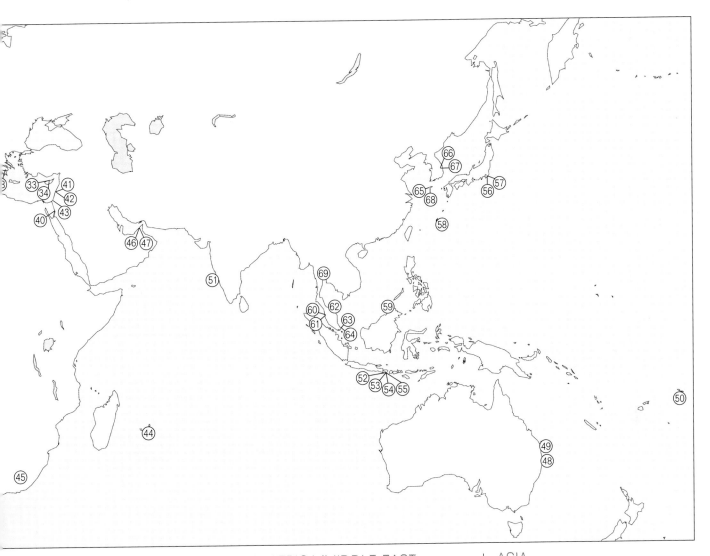

EUROPE/UNITED KINGDOM

Cyprus
(33) Aphrodite Inter-Continental Resort Hotel 56
(34) Le Meridien Limassol Spa & Resort 209
England
(35) Claridge's 64
France
(36) Disneyland® Hotel at DISNEYLAND® Paris 212
Greece
(37) Alatas Island Resort 54
(38) Regency Casino Thessaloniki 100
Spain
(39) Hyatt Regency La Manga 168

AFRICA/MIDDLE EAST

Egypt
(40) Taba Hotel Sofitel 57
Jordan
(41) Grand Hyatt Amman 84
(42) Hotel Inter-Continental Jordan 78
(43) Mövenpick Resort & Spa Dead Sea 162
Mauritius
(44) Le Saint Géran 134
South Africa
(45) The Palace of The Lost City 101
United Arab Emirates
(46) Emirates Hills Villa Estates 150
(47) Royal Mirage 46

ASIA

Australia
(48) Chevron Renaissance 87
(49) Hyatt Regency Coolum 176
French Polynesia
(50) Hotel Bora Bora 126
India
(51) The Leela Palace, Goa 34
Indonesia
(52) Grand Hyatt Bali 16
(53) Le Meridien Nirwana Golf & Spa Resort 208
(54) Nikko Bali Resort & Spa 40
(55) The Ritz-Carlton, Bali 50
Japan
(56) Four Seasons Hotel Tokyo at Chinzan-so 60
(57) Lotte World Tokyo 222
(58) Palm Hills Golf Resort 196
Malaysia
(59) Borneo Resort Karambunai 55
(60) Mandarin Oriental, Kuala Lumpur 66
(61) Palace of the Golden Horses 214
(62) Tanjong Jara Resort 138
Singapore
(63) Merchant Court Hotel, Singapore 86
(64) Shangri-La Hotel, Garden Wing 80
South Korea
(65) Hotel Lotte Cheju Resort 26
(66) Kangwon Casino Resort 117
(67) Oak Valley Destination Resort 158
(68) The Shilla, Cheju 216
Thailand
(69) The Regent of Bangkok 74

Alphabetical Index / Credits

Contributing Authors

Scott Burlingame

Scott Burlingame is editor and publisher of *Vacation Ownership World* magazine, an independent trade periodical that has covered the timesharing industry since the early 1970s. He has an undergraduate degree from U.C. Berkeley and an advanced degree in economics from the University of Copenhagen.

Marshall A. Calder

Marshall A. Calder is managing director of The Leading Small Hotels of the World, Ltd, which was launched on behalf of travelers seeking the personalized luxury of a smaller hotel and the security associated with a global brand. Mr Calder's vast experience in the luxury hotel market includes serving as president of Prima Hotels, a subsidiary of Hotel Representative, Inc.

Sol Kerzner

Sol Kerzner is chairman and chief executive officer of Sun International Hotels Limited, whose landmarks include Atlantis, Paradise Island in the Bahamas, and The Lost City in South Africa. Mr Kerzner is the recipient of numerous honors for his contributions to the hotel industry over the last 40 years and is credited with revolutionizing the casino resort industry in sub-Saharan Africa and, now, throughout the world.

Rowan Moore

Rowan Moore is the architecture critic of the *London Evening Standard*. He was formerly editor of *Blueprint* and a founding partner of Zombory Moldovan Moore Architects. Mr Moore has written books on Tate Modern, Norman Foster, and Nicholas Grimshaw and was the editor and principal author of *Vertigo, the Strange New World of the Contemporary City*. He broadcasts and lectures frequently on architecture.

Richard L. Ragatz, PhD

Richard L. Ragatz, PhD, is executive vice president of RCI Consulting and a leading market researcher and consultant in the vacation home industry. He has been involved in over 1,000 studies in 26 countries on behalf of resort developers and lenders. In 1995, Mr Ragatz was named Industry Leader of the Year by the American Resort Development Association.

Michael S. Rubin, PhD

Michael S. Rubin, PhD, is president of MRA International and chairman of MRA Eventures, specializing in entertainment-based development. Mr Rubin is involved in the development of new sports-based, music-based, movie-themed, internet-based, and media-based attractions throughout the United States. He is vice-chair of ULI's Entertainment Development Council and co-author of *Developing Urban Entertainment Centers*.

Mary Scoviak-Lerner

Mary Scoviak-Lerner is the design editor of *HOTELS* magazine, an international business publication for the hotel industry. Ms Scoviak-Lerner also serves as executive editor of *HOTELS' Investment Outlook*, a magazine for the international hotel investment community, and is author of the book *International Hotel and Resort Design*.

Isadore Sharp

Isadore Sharp is chairman and chief executive officer of Four Seasons Hotels and Resorts. From the time he founded the company in 1960, Mr Sharp has worked to establish Four Seasons as the world's premier luxury hospitality company. Four Seasons Hotels and Resorts currently manages luxury properties in over 30 countries.

Judy Singer

Judy Singer is president of The Spa Resource Group (SRG), which provides management services for resorts, hotels, health clubs, and freestanding spas. She is also a principal in Health Fitness Dynamics, Inc. (HFD), which works with fine hotels, resorts, and mixed-use developments to plan and manage service-oriented profit center health spas. Ms Singer is the chairperson of the International Society of Hospitality Consultants.

Véronique Vienne

Véronique Vienne writes a monthly column for *House & Garden* magazine, is a contributing writer for *Architectural Record*, and is the author of *The Art of Doing Nothing* and *The Art of Imperfection*. Ms Vienne was born in Paris, trained at the Paris Beaux-Arts School of Architecture, and currently works from Brooklyn, New York.

Jana Wolff

Jana Wolff has written for and about design professionals for over 20 years. A published author who is most often a ghostwriter, she wrote the project descriptions in this book and was a principal contributor to a previous collection of the firm's work, entitled *The Hospitality and Leisure Architecture of Wimberly Allison Tong & Goo*. Ms Wolff's recent writings have appeared in *The New York Times*, *Host* magazine, *Chicago Tribune*, and *Honolulu* magazine.

Collaborators

The following past and present employees of WATG helped to make the projects in this book a reality.

Peer Abben
Renee Abdessalam
Dean Abernathy
Raymond Abeyta
Doug Ackerman
John Ackerman
Alberto Acuna
Catherine Adachi
Donald Adams
Jennifer Adams
Ernesto Agaloos, Jr.
Ellen Agcaoili
Jose Luis Ahumada
Peter Aiello
Lois Ajifu
Melvin Ako
Peter Akran
Stephen Albert
Bryan Algeo
Wais Karim Ali
Mike Allen
Gerald Allison
Lynn Allison
David Alsop
Lori Ann Amaki
Sharrise Amlani
Takahashi Ande
Patrick Andersen
Mary Anderson
Lorrin Andrade
Cecilia Angulo
Charles Apel
Homeyra Arbabi
Storm Archer III
Gretchen Arnemann
Alma Arnold
Bernardo Artola
Rashid Ashraf
Jennifer Asselstine
Chad Asuncion
Charlotte Atkinson
Bunny Au
Charissa Au
William Au
Leticia Avalos
Lindon Bachelder
Fely Baisac
Michael Bakemore
Jim Balding
Robert Baldino
Pam Baldwin
Ronald Banco
Scott Barbour
Jill Barclay
Dan Barlev
Lell Barnes
Dee Bartlett
Sandra Barzilay
Gilbert Basbas
Roy Bass
Rodney Batara
Michael Batchelor
Luis Beckford
Christopher Belknap
David Bell
Paul Belle
Eusebio Bello
Kristina Benkovsky
Marcia Benson
George Berean
David Berggren
Maureen Bergin
Ruben Betancourt
Josette Bevirt

Sylvia Beyke
John Bigay
Andrea Binikos
Randy Bishop
Tom Black
Catherine Blackburn
Carla Bloom
Harold Bock
Boanerges Bolanos
Ewa Bolesta
Deberoh Booher
Thanu Boonyawatana
Richard Bosch
Stephen Bossart
Lysanne Bourgouin
Nathalie Boyero
Cynthia Boyle
Robert Boyle
Gordon Bradley
Cary Brockman
Penelope Brocksen
Judi Bronnert
Alex Brostek
Dorothy Brown
Perry Brown
Rebecca Brown
Samuel Brown
Victoria Brown
William Brown
Jerry Browning
Patricia Browning
Michael Brownlie
Kelly Bruce
Cara Brunk
Joseph Bruno
Keith Bryant
Samuel Budiono
Jim Burba
Ian Burgess
Kevin Burt
Shon Burton
Bonifacio Butardo
Dale Butler
C. E. Bye
Dedicacion Cabreros
Naidah Cabrido
Carolyn Calame
Michael Calame
Dean K. Caldarelli
Bertine Callow
Lucas Camacho
Phillip Camp
Thomas Cannon
Christine Cano
Christy Canter
Neil Capangpangan
Roberto Caragay
Jennifer Caravalho
Sarah Cardoza
Beth Carlson
Bradley Carlson
Lisa-Maree Carrigan
Tamara Carroll
Samuel Carson
Elise Carter
Oscar Castelo
Paz Castelo
Cesar Castillo
Richard Cerezo
Curtis Chan
Candis Chang
Henry Chang
Spencer Chang
Sidney Char

Robin Chard
Chau-Hsin Chen
Janie Chen
Jenny Chen
Sam Chen
Sung-Cheng Chen
Feona Cheng
Rachel Chesterfield
Norman Cheung
Sharon Ching
Ion Chiose
Nancy Chitwood
Tat (Alex) Cho
Owen Chock
Sunny Choi
Canossa Choy
Mel Choy
David Christensen
Scott Christensen
Brandishea Christian
Catherine Chun
Kathleen Chun
Kevin Chun
Michael Chun
Carol Chun-Craddock
Terrance Cisco
Jackie Clark
Rachel Clark
Nina Claro-Cuyong
Jill Claus
Peter Clement
Christine Cline
Doug Cochran
Keith Cockett
Adam Coghill
Gregory Coghill
G. Cole
David Coloma
Deanna Cone
Marie Connell
Walter Connors
Howard Cook
P. Cook
Meg Corbett
Jonathan Cort
Charles Corwin
Arnel Costa
Mazeppa Costa
Page Costa
Robert Costa
Cheryl Costello
Robert Cox
Cheryl Creber
Virginia Criley
Keith Crockett
Robert Crone
John Cropper
Mildred Crowson
Monica Cuervo
Howard Culbreth II
Fiona Cumming
Lawrence Cunha
David Curry
Sandra Czerniak-Bye
Lizabeth Czerniel
Michael Czoik
Michelle D'Amico
Rachan Danaphongse
Zohreh Daneshvar
David Daniels
Melanie Daniels
Cary Dasenbrock
Leon David
Tom David

Scott Davis
Patrick Dawson
Robert Day
Andrea De Camp
Thomas De Costa
Kathie De Leon
Maurice De Leon
Polly DeBlank
Thomas Deem
Paul Degenkolb
Cida Deguchi
Jeanette Deighan
Iluminada Delos Santos
Jill Den Hartog
Dan DeSelm
Jessica Dessing
Paolo Diaz
J. Ascenzo Digiacomo
David Dike
Rodrigo Dimla
John Dixon
Travis Do
Dimitri Dobrescu
Susie Dobson
Janice Doering
Robert Dollar
Stephanie Domingo
Shaun Drummond
Francois Du Toit
Kathryn Dunker
Gerald Dunn
Anna Dutton
Jesus Eballar
John Edwards
Karen Eichman
Divina Elefante
Michael Eliades
John Elliott
Kelsey Elliott
Marina Ellison-Nyerges
Suzette Emerson
Maggie Emery
Holly Enete
Kurtis Eng
Scott Ericson
Laura Escarcega
Sherry Eshenbaugh
Erin Espeland
Raul Espiritu
Ilustre Estrella
Rosauro Eva, Jr.
Manuel Evalle
Anna Marie Evans
Scott Ezer
Bruce Fairweather
Donald Fairweather
Thomas Fee
Leslie Feeney
Marjory Feher
David Fellows
Wenfei Feng
Gerald Ferguson
Augusto Fernandez
Laura Fernandez
Ruby Fernandez
Doug Fesler
Jenni Field
Bryan Figuered
Krista Findlay
Steve Fischer
Al Fisher
Jean Fisher
Joni Fisher
Lee Ann Fleming

Bryan Flores
Thomas Fo
Randall Fong
Lynne Ford
Monica Forsyth
Leilani Fortuno
Lorraine Foster
Robert Fox
Emmanoel Francisco
Mary Ann Frank
James Freeman
Susan Frieson
Dean Fukawa
Arnold Fukunaga
Jay Fulton
Louis Fulton
Jason Fung
Vince Fusco
Al Gabay
Jeff Feng Gao
Julie Garcia
Karen Garcia
Jennifer Gardner
Rosemarie Garganta
Neil Garratt
Howard Garris
Michael Ray Garris
Roger Gaspar
Mary Gaudet
Ursula Gehrmann
Patricia Geminell
Natalie Geue
Celia Geyer
Sara Geyer
Robert Gibson
Emma Gibson-Smith
Gary Gidcumb
Sandra Giorgetti
Patrick Girvin
Christopher Go
Lisa Gobeo
Richard Gomez
Cathy Gonzales
Maria Gonzales
Barbara Goo
Debbie Goo
Donald Goo
Wayne Goo
Tina Goodwin
Alexander Gordon
John Gould III
James Grady
Renate Granitzer
Andrea Grassi
Frank Gratton
Deeann Gray
Deborah Green
Georgette Green
Andreas Grieg
Pamela Gring
Gail Gronau-Brown
Jim Gueguierre
Andrë Guerrero
William Gulstrom
Neil Haarhoff
Mary Haase
Thomas Haeg
Marian Haggerty
Tanya Hagiwara
N. Robert Hale
Craig Hall
Sara Hall
Liz Hallin
Brendan Halloran

Simeon Halstead
Nicole Hammond
Elaine Han
James Handsel
George Handy
Cheri Hanna
Shaun Hannah
Edith Hara
John Harada
Diane Hardie
Ian Harris
Norman Harris
Fritz Harris-Glade
Engel Harrop
Horace Hartman
James Harty
Mildred Harvey
Nazie Hashemi
Mark Hastert
David Hayes
Edward Haysom
Gregory Hee
Larry Helber
David Henderson
Francine Henderson
Pamela Hendrickson
Alice Henselman
Felicia Herrick
Jeremy Heyes
Betty Hickok
John Hicks
Elizabeth Higa
Mark Higa
Jack Highwart
Lois Hiram
Ray Hirohama
Wendy Hisashima
Sheila Hixenbaugh
Lawrence Ho
Kim Hoite
Ronald Holecek
Katherine Hollingsworth
Lars Holm
Yu Hong
Ila Hoopai
Cynthia Hope
Carol Hopkins
James Horman
Charles Horne
Mike Hounslow
Anne Hritzay
Dawn Hubbard
M. Hueftle
Bent Huld
Bryant Humann
Mavis Hunnisett
Heber Hurd
Brian Husting
Concepcion Ibanez
Susan Ings
Arkanit Intarajit
Puangthong Intarajit
Robert Iopa
Ra'ana Islam
Rafique Islam
Cynthia Jacobs
Joseph Jacobs
Ruben Jaictin
Tammy James
Cristina Janigan
Monika Jaroszonek
Kenneth Jenkins
Sih-Young Jeon
Dae Soo Ji
Derry-Lynn John
Francis Johnson

James Johnson
Jennifer Johnson
Jon Johnson
Lon Johnson
Lynne Johnson
Michael Johnson
Nilda Johnson
Paul Jones
Debra Joyce
Natalia Juliano
Neil Kahn
Carole Kajiwara
Kenneth Kajiwara
Christine Kakour
Christian Kaleiwahea
Shirley Kanahele
Laura Kanazawa
Daniel Kanekuni
Anne Kanemoto
Denise Kaneshiro
Jason Kaneshiro
Kay Kaneshiro
William Kanotz
Stephanie Kapanui
Alexa Kapioltas
Judith Kaplan
Barry Karim
Milan Karlovac
Kim Karmozyn
Mark Kasarjian
Ken Kashimoto
Mina Kato
Susan Cain Katz
Dean Kawamura
Nancy Au Kawanoue
Stanley Kawasaki
Steven Kearns
Reyna Keaunui
Rosemary Keefe
Lee Kellum
Nicky Kelly
Kathleen Kelm
Nils Kenaston
Kelley Kesinger
Gregory Kessler
Sunchai Keuysuvan
Francik Khalili
Rumman Khan
Ashley Kim
Brandon Kim
David Kim
Dennis Kim
Naomi Kim
Sophia Kim
Glenn Kimura
Lucille Kimura
Pamela Kisow
Anton Kisselgoff
Robert Kleinkopf
Jeanie Kleuter
Chris Knight
Hideo Kobayashi
Laureen Kodama
Jan J. Kofranek
Marcella Kofranek
Justin Koizumi
Ellery Komenaka
Olivier Koning
Richard Koob
Karl Korth
Koizumi Kotaro
George Koteles
Charlene Kowblick
Mikako Koyama
Dorothy Krause
Connie Kruayai

Jon Krueger
Stanley Kruse
Colleen Kunishige
Caroline Kuo
Leslie Kurasaki
Ronald Kwan
Henry Kwok
Kevin La
Gary Lacno
Joan LaFountaine
Devin Lai
Amy Lam
Clemson Lam
Sharon Lang
James Langan
Robert Larsen
Ingrid Larsson
Charles Lau
Elena Lau
Johnny Lau
Marianne Lau
J. Patrick Lawrence
C. Lawson
Leonilo Laxa
Khoi Le
Leslie Le Bon
Anna Lee
Chang Lee
Darren Lee
Donald Lee
Edna Lee
Gary Lee
Hideko Tanaka Lee
Joann Lee
Lisa Lee
Tiffany Lee
Yo Han Lee
Mary Ellen Lenander
Cindy Lenart
Pedrito Leong
John Leopardi
Karen Levesque
Feliciano Libao
Bob Liebsack
Jennifer Lien
Lori Liermann
Thomas Lim
John David Lindsay
Tom Litaker
Marc Lizama
Romela Lloren-Talusan
Christopher Lloyd
James Loftis
Betty Loh
Enrique Lopez
Harold Lopez
Daniel Loriot
Carolyn Loughrey
Noland Lucas
Jose Luciano
John Ludlow
Herb Luke
Sherilyn Lum
Kyle Lung
Paul Lyons
Nilo Mabunay
Deborah Mace
Marcia Mack
Ross Mackenzie
Maureen MacKinnon
Jeffrey MacNeill
Maureen Madigan
R. Maeda
Keith Maekawa
Lynden Maekawa
Robby Mago

Edgardo Mallari
Matius Mandolang
Rohit Mankar
Thomas Manok
Mohamed Mansour
Rocky Marquez
Cynthia Marr
Bude Martin
Christin Martinelli
Eduardo Martinez
Harvey Maruya
F. Marvin
Sharrise Masaki
Michelle Masuda
Eric Matsumoto
John Matsumoto
Toshiko Matsushita
Robert Mattox
R. Mau
Ross Maxwell
Stephanie May
Fayez Mazid
Richard McAllister
Roberta McCabe
Greg McCants
J. Marie McCormick
Martha McCullough
Victoria McDonald
Muriel McGrath
Peter McGurk
Michael McKay
Diane McLeod
Rueko McNally
Bradford McNamee
John McQuown
Karen Mead
Vicki Meece
Louise Mellish
Tony Menezes
Shirley Mercado
Nina Merrell
Caralyn Merrill
Elaine Metler
B. Meyers
Lauren Michioka
Svetlana Micic
Diane Midgely
John Miesen
Fred Mikawa
Vicki Millard
Karen Miller
Kim Mills
Michael Milo, Jr.
Peggy Minger-McCants
Mohamed Mirza
Linda Mitchell
Ronald Mitchell
Ron Mitori
Tom Mitrano
Gary Miyakawa
Carrie Miyasato
Janice Miyoshi-Vitarelli
Sharon Mizuno
Dale Moen
Susan Moises
D. Molegraaf
Hoover Monleon
Frank Montillo
David Moore
James Moore
Brenda Moors
Milford Moralde
Ernesto Morales
Susan Morgan
Steven Morita
Adam Morris

Doug Morris
Mitchell Morris
Jafar Mosleh
Bruce Mosteller
Marie Mundheim
Alan Murakami
Grant Murakami
Craig Murayama
Virginia Murison
Hal Murphy
Julia Murphy
James Murray
Richard Myers
Clint Nagata
Jann Nagato
Ronald Nakagawa
Mark Nakahira
Stephen Nakamitsu
Jeffrey Nakamura
Liane Nakamura
William Nakayama
John Naleyanko
Dayna Nam
Nadi Nammar
Rose Ann Nash
Nevine Nasser
Sally Nava
Paul Nelson
Stephen Nemeth
Carly Nesbitt
Deepak Neupane
Jennifer Neupane
Lester Ng
Ivy Ngeow
Nick Nguyen
Son Nguyen
Amauri Nicasio
Paul Niiyama
Darrell Nilles
Lindsay Nishii
Nancy Nishikawa
Robin Nishimura
Homero Nishiwaki
Timothy Nomer
Bill Nord
Darryl Nordstrom
Pamela Norton
Andrew Nyerges
Homer Oatman
Laura Oatman
Leonora Obispo
Carol Ann Ogata
Terri Olsen
Jean Olvey
Dawn Onaga
Christine Optiz
Merrilee Orcutt
Katherine Orthman
Ernest Oshiro
Tracy G. Oshiro
Scott Osterhage
Scott Ostrowski
Lori Oumaye
Gilbert Oviedo
Linda Owens
Alison Pace
Emily Pagliaro
Perla Palombo
Charlie Palumbo
Michael Paneri
Christina Pang
Rolando Panganiban
Carrie Pannick-Reyes
James Paresi
James Park
John Park

Deborah Parks
N. Parnes
Mark Paskill
Ramesh Patel
Purnima Patil-McCutcheon
Geoff Patterson
E. Duff Paulsen
Daniel Paun
Ilie Paun
Robert Payan
Bernard PeBenito
Noe Pegarido
Chun-Yen Peng
Joe Peng
Rachel Penn
Troy Pennington
Anne Perez
M. Perry
Jon Pharis
Richard Phillips
Apinant Phuphatana
Gordon Pickering
Andrea Piper
Catherine Pollock
Catherine Pollock
Udom Pongsawat
Susan Poole
Daniel Popovici
Allan Porter
Jack Potamianos
Kirk Potter
Azita Pourmehr-Quon
Nick Poynton
Darmawan Prawirohardjo
Vic Preuveneers
Stacy Prince
Brian Prock
John Pugh
Daniel Pun
Shirley Pyun
Angela Quiason
Manolo Quiason
Tricia Quiason
Teresa Quincey
Tina Quintana
Suzanne Rabey
Kay Radzik
Anthony Ramirez
Mariano Ramirez
Carl Ramos
Humberto Ramos
Lori Rapport
Vikki Raschbacher
Guy Ratcliffe
Marcelino Raza
Bruce Reay
Scott Redfield
Emma Redor
William Reed
Nancy Reno
Art Reola
Victoria Reventas
Heather Reynolds
Nathaneal Richards
Sarah Richardson
Carol Rieck
Paul Ries
Jennie Ringer
Daniel Riordan
Andre Riou
Scott Robart
Barry Robinson
Keith Robishaw
Eduardo Robles

Victor Robles
Larry Rocha
David Rodrigues
Kimberly Rodrigues
Gabriel Rodriguez
J. Lee Rofkind
Deborah Rogger
Elizabeth Rosas
Michael Rosen
Deborah Rosenblum
Katherine Rothrock
Donal Rounds
Rosemary Rowan
Hanna Rude
Pamela Rudin
Prudencio Rumbaoa
Lotte Rundqvist
Patrick Russel
Tom Russell
Lila Ruzicka
Helen Ryan
Jeff Sabini
Edie Sagarang
Dennis Sagucio
Ray Sagun
Tatsuo Saito
Wendell Sakagawa
Gregorio Salinas, Jr.
Richard Salvato
Daniel Sandomire
Patrick Sanjongco
Nemencio Santos
Reynaldo Santos
Dennis Sapphire
Atilano Saradpon
Ting Saradpon
Daniel Sauerbrey
Marios Savopoulos
Helen Saw
Robert Schaeffer
Dorothy Schafer
Anna Schef
Thomas Schmidt
James Schmit
Helen Schofield
Kevin Scholl
Jennifer Scott
Peter Scott
Patti Seay
Lydia Seeley
Peter Seo
Yosesh Seth
Beth Shafer
Jayna Shah
Pankaj Shah
Leslie Shammas
Ali Shams
Donald Shaw
Ralph Shelbourne
Brett Shepperson
Dennis Sheridan
Han Shi
Emi Shiga
Vincent Shigekuni
Colin Shimokawa
Janine Shinoki
Dale Shishido
Douglas Shoemaker
David Shu
Eduardo Silva
Jennifer Silva
Charles Sims
Crispolo Sindiong
B. Skadsheim
Paul Slater
Thomas Smail

Curetis Smith
Darren Smith
Eric Smith
Lisa Smith
Maica Smith-Belknap
Valentine Snell
Thomas Snodgrass
Mitzi Snyder
Maria Solomon-Hirao
Norman Soohoo
Brian Spahr
Robert Stempner
Jan Stenberg
Angelica Stern
Robert Stern
Sandy Stern
Cindy Stewart
Amy Stillman
Timothy Stoaks
Stella Stojic
Ivory Chris Stokes
Jennifer Strafford
Audrey Strapple
L. Strauss
Martin Stuart
Karl Stumpf
Lloyd Sueda
Karen Suenaga
Mary Suenaga
Jeanne Sullivan
Sham Summan
David Sung
John Suska
Patrick Sutton
Robert Sutton
Douglas Swank
Arlyn Sweesy
Glenn Sweesy
Garrett Tagawa
Elissa Tajon
Craig Takahata
Stanley Takaki
Gerald Takano
Dorene Takenaka
Joni Takenaka
Serenity Talbot
Joyce Tamanaha
Keith Tamura
Vince Tamura
Xiaosi Tan
Dennis Tarampi
Jackie Tarrant
Susan Tasaki
Ann Tashiro
Chantelle Tate
Mark Tawara
Brett Taylor
Thomas Tengan
Evelyn Tenorio
Alan Teoh
Nestor Terrill
Cliff Terry
Clark Thiel
John Steven Thiersch
James Thomassen
Mark Thomassen
Andrew Thompson
Ann Thompson
Enwood Thompson
Nigel Thorsby
Robert Tindall
Henry Ting
Lisa Tokumaru
Sharie Tokumoto
G. Tokuno
Joann Toledo

Mike Toma
Brett Tomer
Cathy Tondelli
Gregory Tong
Reynaldo Torres
Randy Totel
Dao Tran
Thuan Tran
Thahn Tat Trinh
Lisa Troke
Shirley Tsang
Cynthia Tsugawa
Justin Tucker
Sean Tully
Ismet Turkalp
Anglier Turner
Terry Tusher
Nile Tuzun
Chris Tyler
Alexander Uahihui
Daniel Ubovich
Yurica Ueda
Thomas Uemoto
Benjamin Ugale
Lex Ulibarri
E. Umemoto
Robert Umemura
Jeanne Ung
Susan Uno
Laura Usherwood
Ronald Uyesugi
Gail Uyetake
Farrokh Vahid
Holly Valentine-Steinhoff
Jason Van Auker
Cheryl Ann Van Berkel
Margot Van Heerden
Richard Van Horn
Ronald Van Pelt
Anthony Van Strauhal
Lisa Varela
John Vargas
Joaquin Vasquez
Leroy Velasquez
Rafael Velazquez
Valerie Velves
Brian Veneble
Marc Ventura
Jon Veregge
Carol Vesco
Rudolfo Victorio
Ricardo Viernes
Roberto Viggayan
Greg Villegas
Maria Villegins
Tracy Vincent
Eric Vinson
Ponn Paul Virulrak
Mark Vogt
Deirdre Vouziers
Jolie Wah
Jennifer Wakazuru
Kimberly Walker
Charles Wallace
Rondi Wallace
Christopher Walling
Hillary 'Lalo' Walsh
Thomas Walsh
Mark Walter
George Walters
Marcy Wang
Sheri Wang
Cheryl Ward
Cindy Wasserman
Eugene Watanabe
Linda Watanabe

Douglas Waterman
Martin Waterman
Leslie Watson
Alisa Weaver
Scott Weaver
Marion Weeber
David Weisberg
John Weitz
Robert Wenkham
Amy Wert
George Whisenand
Loy Whisenand
Sabine White
Mark Whitehouse
Shanita Wiggins
Michelle Willey
Darlene Williams
Eugene Williams
Michael Williams
Soh-Hyon Wilson
Suzanne Wilson
George 'Pete' Wimberly
Heather Wimberly
Airie Wise
Tom Witaker
Howard Wolff
Willard Won
Miranda Wong
Robert Wong
Stanley Wong
Flora Wong Chang
David Woo
Tom Wooge
Steven Worthington
Michelle Wright
Henry Thanh Wu
Jay Wu
Thelma Wurm
Charles Wyse
Kurt Xu
Serena Xu
Dani Yafuso
Jennifer Yagi
Dean Yama
Clarice Yamada
Jan Yamamoto
Ross Yamamoto
Roy Yamamoto
Corinne Yamasaki
Brett Yamashita
Maggie Yan
Jia Yao
Chew Leng Yap
Lican Ying
Catherine Yohn
Ross Yokoyama
Kevin Yoneda
Robert Yoneoka
Soo-Hyun Yoon
Logan Yoshida
Mark Yoshizaki
Kellie Yost
Nancy Yost
Allison Young
Kevin Young
Lawrence Young
Lori Young
Richard Young
Donna Yuen
Martin Zauruskas
Sorin Zdrahal
Amor Zendejas
Chao 'Robert' Zheng
Donald Ziebell
Kelly Ziegler
Hongliang Zou

Acknowledgments

Howard J. Wolff
WATG Senior Vice President

On behalf of WATG, thanks go to several key groups of people:

- To WATG clients, who honor us by assigning their dreams to our drawing boards (and computers).

- To WATG staff, who work tirelessly to delight people they will never see.

- To the dozens of fine photographers whose images bring these pages to life.

- To the talented professionals from the many design, engineering, and construction firms with whom we collaborate.

Several individuals deserve special thanks, as well:

Jan Stenberg worked diligently to gather project information and verify the accuracy of all that is contained in this book. She was assisted by Chao Robert Zheng, Cindy Wasserman, Debra Joyce, Olivier Koning, Mazeppa Costa, Dave Lindsay, Chad Asuncion, and Lalo Walsh.

Last and first thanks go to Paul Latham and Alessina Brooks at The Images Publishing Group, who thought our work was worthy of such an immodest title.

Every effort has been made to trace the original source of copyright material contained in this book. The publishers would be pleased to hear from copyright holders to rectify any errors or omissions.

The information and illustrations in this publication have been prepared and supplied by Wimberly Allison Tong & Goo. While all reasonable efforts have been made to source the required information and ensure accuracy, the publishers do not, under any circumstances, accept responsibility for errors, omissions and representations express or implied.

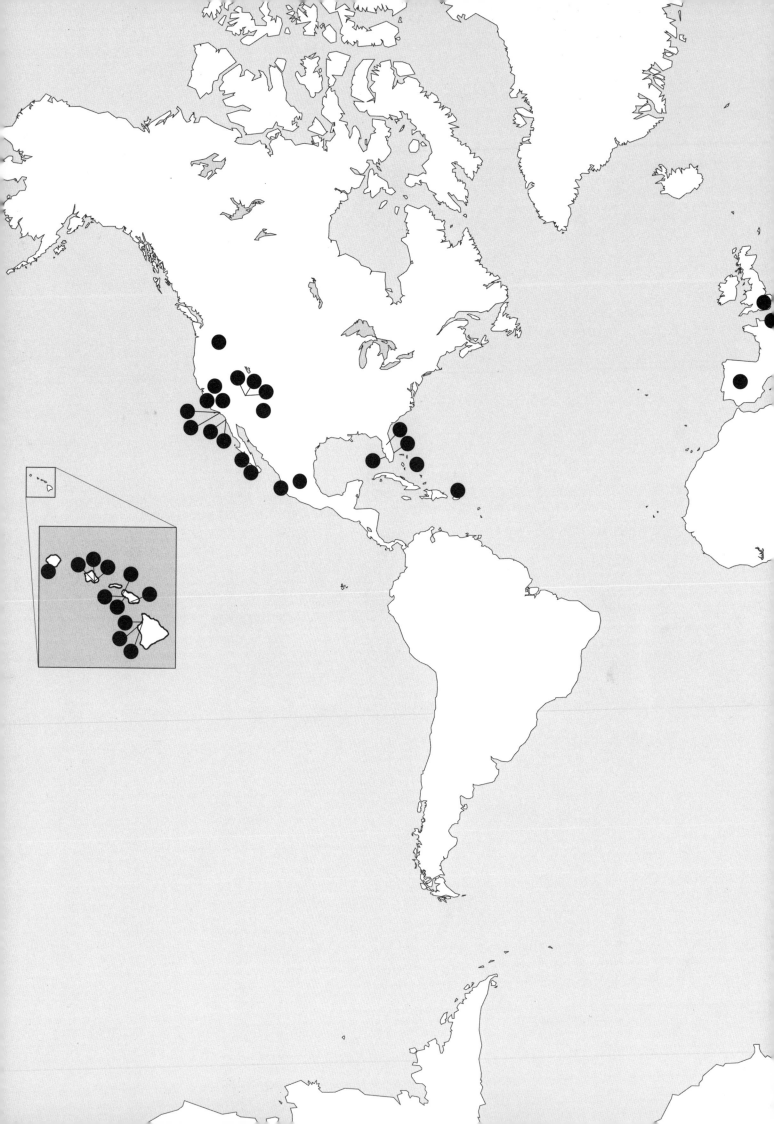